WITHDRAWN
10655821

SOME STUDIES IN THE MODERN NOVEL

SOME STUDIES IN
THE MODERN NOVEL

Dorothy M. Hoare
Fellow and Associate of Newnham College, Cambridge

1938
CHATTO & WINDUS
LONDON

PUBLISHED BY
Chatto & Windus
LONDON
*
The Macmillan Company
of Canada, Limited
TORONTO

To

Gertrude Caton-Thompson

with admiration

Contents

AUTHOR'S NOTE

MOST of these essays were delivered as lectures in the English Faculty at Cambridge : I have thought it best not to alter them too much in re-casting, preferring to retain something of the vitality of the spoken word.

I record with pleasure my indebtedness to my friends Mrs. N. K. Chadwick and Miss Enid Welsford for the stimulus of their encouragement and criticism, and to Newnham College for its generous support with publication.

Acknowledgments are due to the Editors of *The New Adelphi*, *The Cambridge Review* and the *Everyman* series, where parts of these essays have appeared.

HENRY JAMES

HENRY JAMES is a writer who is capable of infinite surprises. For instance between Henry James and Virginia Woolf, perhaps the most modern of the modern novelists, there is an affinity of technique and to some extent of subject matter. Yet Henry James began writing in the seventies, a period which it is true produced Gerard Manley Hopkins but which also produced Ruskin, Rossetti, Morris, whose work one would hesitate to call distinctly "contemporary." "Contemporary" is however the adjective which I think we shall find ourselves finally applying to Henry James.[1]

Again, there is no one about whom critical prejudice

[1] And it has of course been applied to him, by Stephen Spender, who in his book *The Destructive Element*, puts forward James as the first communist. I should state that my remarks on James [given first as a lecture some time before Mr. Spender's book appeared, and substantially unchanged since] have found corroboration from his opinions there. I cannot however agree with all of Mr. Spender's views on James, particularly on his communism. I would say that James' insistence on a personal morality which very often is not the conventional one indicates his awareness of the insecurity of his social world and may be taken as an indirect criticism of it; for of course in an ideal society personal and social moral values would not be at variance. This is however as far as I should wish to go. Anything as anarchical as communism would have been antipathetic to James, in my opinion.

has been more definitely pre-conceived. Until very recently, if one had asked anyone who had not made a very close study of the novels or gone to most of the writers who had, for an opinion, the general criticism disengaged would have been one of arid intellectual web-spinning. "That ingenious spider weaving his webs . . . to me he had no appeal," said Jane Harrison. Similarly E. M. Forster voices what one might call the general intellectual attitude to James, in *Aspects of the Novel*. There he points out one of the aspects of James' work which has always been singled out for attention. "Many readers," he says, "cannot grant his premise, which is that most of human life has to disappear before he can do us a novel." A very damning indictment. And again, in a brilliant image, "No social explanation of the world we know is possible (for James' characters), for there are no stupid people in their world, no barrier of language, and no poor. Even their sensations are limited. Maimed creatures can alone breathe in Henry James' pages—maimed yet specialized. They remind one of the exquisite deformities who haunted Egyptian art in the reign of Akhnaton—huge heads, and tiny legs, but nevertheless charming. In the following reign they disappear."

And finally, this time coming right out in the open with his charge—"There is no philosophy in the novels, no religion (except an occasional touch of superstition), no prophecy, no benefit for the superhuman at all. It (the maiming of human life) is for the sake of a particular aesthetic effect, which is certainly gained, but at this price."

It is easy to dispose of the first objection, by admitting

that a great deal of it is true but not necessarily derogatory —"there are no stupid people in his world, no barrier of language, and no poor." To that extent it is admittedly an artificial world. Theodora Bosanquet, who worked with Henry James in his latter years as his secretary, says some excellent and penetrating things in one of the Hogarth essays.[1] "By 1909, the men and women of Henry James could talk only in the manner of their creator. His own speech, assisted by the practice of dictating, had by that time become so inveterately characteristic that his questions to a railway clerk about a ticket or to a fishmonger about a lobster, might easily be recognized as coined in the same mint as his addresses to the Academic Committee of the Royal Society of Literature." And again, "To be 'inarticulate' was for him the cardinal social sin. It amounted to a wilful withholding of treasures of alien experience. . . . (Such) numerous (inarticulate) persons he dismissed from his attention as 'simple organisms.' These he held to be mere waste of any writer's time." These remarks are corroborated by a letter written from Italy in 1874, where Henry James complains that he has had no stimulus worth mentioning for over a year, for the only people he had talked to were washerwomen and waiters, both coming into the category of "simple organisms," and therefore useless to the literary man.

Admittedly, in James' world there are no stupid people, no barriers of language, and no poor. Yet is this statement which Forster uses as a means of condemnation, anything more than a negative way of describing the

[1] *Henry James at Work.* Hogarth Essays, 3. London, 1924.

limits which James imposed on his work? We are here in much the same position as we should be in defending Wordsworth from the charge of inanity in the *Lyrical Ballads*.

But of course Forster's charge goes deeper than that, and his second objection is more difficult to meet, namely, the exclusive interest in technique. This indeed seems to be borne out by Henry James himself, for in one of his letters written to H. G. Wells, he says: "It is art that *makes* life, makes interest, makes importance . . . and I know of no substitute whatever for the force and beauty of its process." But there is an immense difference between being interested in form or pattern as a means to an end, and being interested in it solely for itself. Nothing is more evident to anyone who knows James' work at all well than that he is intensely interested in pattern, more indeed than he is in his characters; but that what governs his interest in both is the idea to be expressed through them. I should like, anticipating my proof, to misquote Forster and say: "The aesthetic is there for a particular *moral* effect." And also to quote from another of James' letters: "My poetic and my appeal to experience rest upon . . . my measure of fulness—fulness of life and of the projection of it. . . . I hold that interest may be, must be, exquisitely made and created, and that if we don't make it, we who undertake to, nobody and nothing will make it for us. . . . Of course for myself I live, live intensely and am fed by life, and my value, whatever it may be, is in my own kind of expression of that . . . the extension of life, which is the novel's best gift."

A curious phrase for the cold formalist of Forster's picture. There are two questions to answer. What kind of *extension of life* do we find in the novels, and what is James' *own kind of expression of that*? The enquiry involves some treatment of the early novels, for they afford a clear indication that the natural and first interest of James was in something very far removed from technical perfection.

I

Roderick Hudson, written in 1875, is a good example of James' early preoccupations, as a bald outline of the story will show. Roderick Hudson, a young American sculptor of enormous promise, is discovered kicking his heels in a New England village by Rowland, a wealthy acquaintance, who is there visiting friends. Rowland takes Roderick with him to Italy, and before they set out, Roderick reveals the fact that he is engaged to be married to Mary Garland, a young, serious quiet girl who anticipates the later Jamesian heroines. In Italy, Roderick rapidly attains great reputation no less on account of his manner which often shows the privileged rudeness of genius, than because of his artistic powers. In due course he meets with Christina Light, a sophisticated, clever, beautiful young girl who makes no secret of the fact that her mother designs her for the most brilliant marriage she can attain. Roderick and she feel the common attraction of a certain strength and lawlessness. They fall in love. At this point Rowland intervenes, on behalf of Mary Garland, to whom it must be observed, he on his side, is silently devoted. Roderick consents to have Mary brought to Rome to counteract Christina's influence.

Christina consents to renounce her influence on Roderick. The plan however does not work. Christina, forced by an unexpected crisis, marries a wealthy and famous Italian prince. Roderick goes to Switzerland; but by mischance Christina also is there, and they meet. That night Roderick spends walking in the mountains: there is a terrific thunderstorm; Roderick does not appear at the inn where Rowland and his friends await him, and in the morning a frenzied search-party find him dead at the foot of a ravine.

Such is the story. It will be obvious how similar this is to the opening theme of *The Ambassadors* (written in 1903), and how very differently James uses his material in the later book. Here the story moves in a leisurely fashion; it has room for descriptions of the artist's reactions to various stimuli, and for conversations on the freedom of an artist's life and its peculiar laws—a theme which finds somewhat different handling in *The Tragic Muse*—a history not of a sculptor but of a great actress. Some of the action, as the plot reveals, is open to the charge of melodrama—a charge again to be levelled at another novel written about the same time, *The American*. In it we have the story of an American business man who dared to aspire to the hand of a French countess; and a murder, a duel, a death-bed confession, and other such ingredients of the normal third-rate thriller are introduced either as vital to the main action or as sub-plot.

It may be objected that it is unfair to produce merely the outline of the plot of any novel, and say that it is highly romantic or even melodramatic. What I should like to stress here is that in *Roderick Hudson* and the early novels generally, the plot *is* important, it is the centre of the book, in a way in which the plot of *The Ambassadors* for example is not. In *The Ambassadors*, action is conspicuous by its absence; there is nothing of the rapid transition from event to event, from spectacular event to event, that there is in *Roderick Hudson* or *The American*. The success of the later book is bound up with what one might call the gradual *weathering* of the character by a series of infinitely small, internal mental exertions, and depends on the subtlety and intricacy of development, and not on the boldness of any external action.

If a typical passage from *Roderick Hudson* is compared with any of the later works, we shall be nearer to the problem of Henry James' art. Here for example is an account of Roderick given to Rowland at the beginning of the book:

> His mother is a widow of a Massachusetts country family, a little timid tremulous woman who is always on pins and needles about her son. She had some property herself and married a Virginia gentleman—an owner of lands and slaves. He turned out, I believe, a dreadful rake, and made great havoc in their fortune. Everything, or almost everything, melted away, including Mr. Hudson himself. This is literally true, for he drank himself to death. Ten years ago his wife was left a widow with scanty means and a couple of growing boys . . . Roderick, our friend, was her pride and joy; but Stephen, the elder, was her comfort and support. I remember him later; he was a plain-faced, sturdy, practical lad, very different from his brother, and in his way I imagine a very fine fellow.

No critic, I imagine, would accuse this kind of writing of being too mannered, nor could one say with truth that there is much interest in technique evinced here. The expression is clumsy and full of clichés, and there is no trace of any precision of statement. It is a piece of writing which one might find in any newspaper, and I quote it merely to show how loose, how *un*formed, how *un*-mannered, James' early work could be. A more interesting example from the same novel is the description of Mary Garland:

> Her face . . . was not . . . a quick and mobile face, over which expression flickered like a candle in the wind. They followed each other slowly, distinctly, sincerely, and you might almost have fancied that, as they came and went, they gave her a sort of pain. She was tall and slender and had an air of maidenly strength and decision. She had a broad forehead and dark eyebrows, a trifle thicker than those of classical beauties; her grey eye was clear but not brilliant and her features were bravely irregular. She wore a scanty white dress, and had a nameless rustic, provincial air.

But what is this reminiscent of? Surely

> She had a rustic woodland air
> And she was wildly clad.

In other words, it recalls the romantic utterance at its height.

One of the first characteristics, then, of the early James, is a strong romantic sensibility, and anyone criticizing *Roderick Hudson*, *The American*, *The Tragic Muse*, would have felt inclined to warn the writer, not of indulgence in too rigid and formal a technique but of the danger of romantic excess, in situation, in sentiment, in description —of loose feeling and loose writing.

Let me now quote a passage from a novel written in

1902, perhaps James' most typical, if not his best—certainly one which reveals all his central characteristics—*The Wings of the Dove*. The passage comes from the opening chapter (a description of the heroine) and may serve very well as a contrast to the portrait of Mary Garland:

> She waited, Kate Croy, for her father to come in, but he kept her unconscionably, and there were moments at which she showed herself in the glass over the mantel, a face positively pale with the irritation that had brought her to the point of going away without sight of him. It was at this point, however, that she remained; changing her place, moving from the shabby sofa to the armchair upholstered in a glazed cloth that gave at once—she had tried it—the sense of the slippery and of the sticky. She had looked at the sallow prints on the walls and at the lonely magazine, a year old, that combined, with a small lamp in coloured glass and a knitted white centre-piece wanting in freshness, to enhance the effect of the purplish cloth on the central table; she had above all from time to time taken a brief stand on the small balcony to which the pair of long windows gave access. . . . Each time she turned in again, each time in her impatience she gave him up, it was to sound a deeper depth, while she tasted the faint flat emanation of things, the failure of fortune and of honour. If she continued to wait it was really in a manner that she mightn't add the shame of fear, of individual, of personal collapse, to all the other shames. To feel the street, to feel the room, to feel the table-cloth and the centre-piece and the lamp, gave her a small salutary sense at least of neither shirking nor lying. This whole vision was the worst thing yet. . . . (But) wasn't it in fact the partial escape from this "worst" in which she was steeped, to be able to make herself out again as agreeable to see? She stared into the tarnished glass too hard indeed to be staring at her beauty alone. She readjusted the poise of her black

> closely feathered hat, retouched, beneath it, the thick fall of her dusky hair; kept her eyes aslant no less on her beautiful averted than on her beautiful presented oval. . . . She was handsome, but the degree of it was not sustained by items and aids; a circumstance moreover playing its part at almost any time in the impression she produced. The impression was one that remained, but as regards the sources of it no sum in addition would have made up the total.

This is an intricate opening to a story which needs very careful balance in the telling. How *full*, in comparison with *Roderick Hudson*, the texture has become—scene, person, atmosphere, mental state, all inter-reacted. In the early novels, much time is wasted in straightforward and naïve description of the kind already quoted [in a sense, there is more room in the early work than in this tightened, close writing; in *The American*, for instance, James finds space for a humorous description of a New England parson, a character put in merely for malicious amusement in type. He has nothing to do with the story, and after his first appearance doesn't recur again. And his portrait in itself is amusing and interesting]. But generally, in the early novels, the lights and shades are not managed well; and if the later James is all a matter of obscure greys, these are much too hard black and white, approaching perilously near the caricature of Victorian melodrama. In the early novels a rambling and discursive method is adopted because as yet he does not know his artistic business. In the later novels, with which I shall most be concerned, all the *apparent* long-windedness is given solely for the purpose of greater accuracy in definition. It is obvious that between *Roderick Hudson* and

The Wings of the Dove there has been a complete change of style, an advance in technique so startling that it almost looks as though technique had become the chief aim. I hope to prove that this is exactly what it had not.

2

Any consideration of the later novels brings out the astonishing fact that they are all, in more or less degree, and with more or less emphasis, saying the same thing. From *The Spoils of Poynton* in 1897 to his last two books written in 1915, we have a series of eight or nine novels (*The Spoils of Poynton*, *What Maisie Knew*, *The Awkward Age*, *The Wings of the Dove*, *The Ambassadors*, *The Golden Bowl*, *The Ivory Tower*, *The Sense of the Past*), admittedly containing the best which James wrote, all of which are *divertissements* on the same theme, and that theme, a matter of what one might call "morality." James knew that morals were important—he is not a New Englander for nothing. At the same time this is not what makes him interesting—it is his peculiar kind of morality, the peculiar, intricate, subtle interplay of feelings and resolutions between his characters, to make up what one might call the Jamesian idea of how to live, that is so remarkable.

I was first very much struck by this by chancing to read three books one after the other, which had been written in close succession—*The Awkward Age* (1899), *The Wings of the Dove* (1902), *The Ambassadors* (1903). From these three books it was evident what James was after. They are all situations of renunciation.

In *The Ambassadors*, for example, the dénouement

comes with the change in Strether's attitude—(he has been sent, one remembers, to Paris as the elderly friend of the family in America, to save Chadwick Newsome from an entanglement with a Frenchwoman)—the dénouement comes with the change in Strether's attitude from desire to bring Chadwick away, free from this intrigue, to not only an acceptance of the situation, but a positive injunction that Chadwick shall stay, though without legal or conventional right, and reward Mme. de Vionnet's services to him with the strictest loyalty. But behind this there is a second situation, even more important to Strether than Chadwick's affairs. His own relationship with his friend and adviser Maria Gostrey, has come to a critical point—she practically offers him her devotion:

> He took a minute to say, for, really and truly, what stood about him there in her offer—which was as the offer of exquisite service, of lightened care, for the rest of his days, might well have tempted. It built him softly round, it roofed him warmly over, it rested, all so firm, on selection.

The final and crucial passage of the book comes with Strether's refusal to permit himself (for it would involve a loss of integrity on his part, his feeling for Mme. de Vionnet being what it is) to accept this offer:

> That, you see, is my only logic. Not, out of the whole affair, to have got anything for myself.

Even more clearly *The Awkward Age* and *The Wings of the Dove* reveal this point. In both the same theme is discussed with slight differentiations, and brought to the same inevitable end. In both there is what might be termed a purification following on trial. In *The*

Wings of the Dove, Merton Densher has to choose between Kate Croy and Milly Theale; in *The Awkward Age*, Van has to decide whether he will marry Nanda to please old Mr. Longdon and to advance his own interests, or not. In both the delicate niceties of conscience and honour are stressed—the individual conscience, it is important to note, and the individual responsibilities (witness for example Kate Croy's compact with Densher). In *The Awkward Age*, Nanda's quivering but resolute abnegation of what she might have—the half-loaf, the crumbs, of Van's affection—is the main thing. What is stressed is the *withdrawal from* something which does not come up to the individual's standard of integrity, of fullness, even although that something is not in itself undesirable. *The Wings of the Dove* and *The Awkward Age* express indeed the same equation in different terms; what it is may best be given in Henry James' own words:

> What I hate is myself—when I think that one has to take so much, to be happy, out of the lives of others, and that one isn't happy even then. . . . What it comes to is that it's not, it's never, a happiness, any happiness at all, to *take*. The only safe thing is to give. . . . (*The Ambassadors.*)

Renunciation of what one knows to be not fully consonant with one's integrity, then, is the very apparent motif of these three books. The problem with which Henry James is concerned is one of very delicately poised behaviour, of very subtly adjusted moral standards. And here we are only at the beginning of his art.

The renunciation in each case comes from a highly intelligent and complex personality, fully aware of what is involved. It is no easy situation with which the Jamesian character is confronted. Like Eliot, like Hopkins, James knows that the only way for the mind to be free is to be master of its desires, to control them by ceasing to have them. The same essential theme underlies his novels as that which underlies Eliot's

> Teach us to care and not to care
> Teach us to sit still,

and, though Hopkins indicates a very different method of approach, the same problem is found in his central poems:

> O in all that coil that toil since, seems, I kiss'd the rod,
> Hand rather, my heart lo! lapped strength, stole joy, would laugh, cheer.

The triumph of individual integrity through intelligent renunciation—let me stress the word intelligent. For it is very noteworthy that the contrast between the subtle spider-like spinning of complicated intertwined situation, and the final severity and plainness of the character's response to the critical moment, is absolutely essential. The complication, the intricacy of situation, is necessary to reveal the importance, the value of the response.

This will emerge by a very simple comparison. In Jane Austen, for example, the question of intricacy does not arise. In showing the reactions of Wentworth and Anne in *Persuasion*, in the admirable accurate description of Anne's feelings in the concert room, Jane Austen has merely to state a certain series of simple observed facts. A perfectly clear and just account of what happens is given—the *superficial* actions are described, and one says, Yes, she is feeling, and feeling intensely.

James is concerned with characters who are much more

critically aware of their own responses, and much more capable of subtle analysis. The interest lies in the analysis almost more than in the first feeling—in the half-shades, the fleeting glimpses of intention and attitude which can never quite be brought out in their full complexity. Generally in James' work, the motive behind action is exceedingly subtle, as in life, and requires to be analysed before it can be evaluated.

3

A somewhat detailed analysis of *The Golden Bowl* may perhaps afford the best instance of what one might call the *integrity* which James stresses, and also of the complications which it involves.

Prince Amerigo, a young impoverished Italian nobleman, marries for the sake of rehabilitating his family fortunes, the wealthy and beautiful Maggie Verver, daughter of Adam Verver an American millionaire. It is on Amerigo's side a marriage *de convenance,* helped by the fact that he likes and respects his wife though he isn't in love with her. Indeed how could he be, when he is very deeply in love with Charlotte Stanton, as she is with him; whom he would have married but for the fact that—in that disinterested and critical way in which Henry James' characters can look on themselves—they both agree that it would be impossible owing to their poverty.

Charlotte, who is a great friend of Maggie's, has been in America but comes over to England in time for the marriage. She and Amerigo, who both have an extraordinary sense of the obligations laid on them by

Amerigo's marriage, steal a last morning together before parting, ostensibly so that Charlotte can buy a wedding-present. They go into a small shop, at the end of a long search, and Charlotte is attracted by a very beautiful crystal bowl, of a gold colour and most exquisite proportions but with an infinitesimal flaw in its structure.

> "Does one make a present" (she asks the shopkeeper) "of an object that contains, to one's knowledge, a flaw?"
>
> "Well, if one knows of it one has only to mention it. . . . The good faith," the man smiled, "is always there."
>
> "And leave the person to whom one gives the thing, you mean, to discover it?"
>
> "He wouldn't discover it, if you're speaking of a gentleman."

And again,

> "Does crystal then break—when it *is* crystal? I thought its beauty was its hardness."
>
> Her friend in his way discriminated. "Its beauty is its *being* crystal. But its hardness is certainly its safety. It doesn't break," he went on, "like vile glass. It splits—if there is a split."

All this is highly symbolical of the general situation, and the image is developed later, as we shall see.

Maggie and the Prince marry: the Prince and her father bound Maggie's horizon. Old Adam Verver begins to wonder, in the hypersensitive fashion of James' characters, whether he had not better marry Charlotte, in order to prevent Maggie—a most devoted daughter—from feeling that by her marriage she has deserted him. Maggie realizes nothing about the Prince's attitude to Charlotte; nor at this point, we assume, does her father.

He has his "grand idea" apparently only on his daughter's behalf.

One cannot at the time quite accept this, *qua* character. The devotion and the remedy seem disproportionate to fact. *We* know that Maggie is as yet untroubled by anything except her father's loneliness. Is it certain that her father is as unaware? That question shifts the balance of attention, but we don't as yet know the answer. It is impossible from the data given by James to form a definite reply—it is his method indeed of keeping the situation freshly before us, of making us realize that there are undercurrents of fears and suspicions, of alterations and adjustments beneath the apparently calm surface.

Charlotte marries Adam, and the situation becomes doubly complicated as the two families are constantly with each other. Maggie and her father show their devotion to each other; Charlotte and the Prince conceal their mutual passion. They vow indeed to treat their respective spouses with a care and tenderness superlative. They agree that, being people of honour, they can trust each other:

> "It's all too wonderful."
>
> Firmly and gravely she kept his hand. "It's too beautiful." And so for a minute they stood together, as strongly held and as closely confronted as any hour of their easier past even had seen them. They were silent at first, only facing and faced, only grasping and grasped, only meeting and met. "It's sacred," he said at last.
>
> "It's sacred," she breathed back at him. They vowed it, gave it out and took it in, drawn, by their intensity, more closely together. Then of a sudden, through this tightened circle as at the issue of a narrow strait into the sea beyond,

everything broke up, broke down, gave way, melted and mingled. Their lips sought their lips, their pressure their response and their response their pressure; with a violence that had sighed itself the next moment to the longest and deepest of stillnesses they passionately sealed their pledge.

After this, of course, the reader knows where he stands. The only person who doesn't know, who remains radiantly confident and happy, is Maggie. But one day she sees in the same shop-window the same golden bowl—and buys it as a present for her father. The shopman comes to tell her that it is cracked (he is certainly not a person of the real world) and innocently relates the visit he had had from the other two prospective buyers, and how their words and attitude to each other had impressed his memory with their obvious infatuation. Incidentally he hopes she has not yet bestowed the crystal bowl, "for," he says, "it wasn't a thing for a present to a person she was fond of, for she wouldn't wish to give a present that would bring ill-luck." The symbolism is again clear; the cracked bowl represents at once the crack in Maggie's faith.

Maggie is now in full possession of the situation—she immediately remembers vague hints, actions, words, which had passed unheeded by her before, and now come home with dreadful force. She puts the bowl on her mantelpiece; one Mrs. Assingham who throughout the book has acted as intimate observer of the situation happens to visit Maggie at this point, and hears all. She takes the bowl in her hand and deliberately dashes it on the floor.

"Whatever you meant by it—and I don't want to know *now*—has ceased to exist," Mrs. Assingham said.

It is important to note here how in most of Henry James' books the presence of a detached observer is necessary, who looks on at the central situation and who by reason of his or her "beautiful intelligence," sorts out the significant fragments and puts them dexterously before the astonished and fascinated eyes of the reader. Mrs. Assingham in this novel, Davey Bradham in *The Ivory Tower*, Strether in *The Ambassadors*, Mr. Longdon in *The Awkward Age*, all are there in order to make awareness more aware, to reveal the growing situation in the clearest possible light. In this respect, Henry James is far behind the method of his closest disciple, Virginia Woolf, who has managed finally to eliminate the observer. It is interesting to reflect that that is a feat, for the psychological novel. Dorothy Richardson eliminates the observer too, but often with disastrous results. Conrad who was in a large part of his work impelled by the same desire as James to show the

> Bonds no man could unbind
> Being imagined within
> The labyrinth of the mind
>
> (Yeats)

also has to use his device. In James' own work I can only think of two novels, *The Sense of the Past* and *What Maisie Knew* (and possibly, though with some qualifications, Strether in *The Ambassadors*), where the intelligent observer is *also* the active participator in the drama, and where the situation gradually unfolds to us through its gradual unfolding in the mind of that person.

But to get back to *The Golden Bowl*. The crack is

apparent—the bowl is smashed. Will the relationship between Maggie and Amerigo, between Amerigo and Charlotte also be broken—that fine fabric which has been woven with such infinite care and pains? Maggie and the Prince at least know that the situation between them is new. That at least the breaking of the bowl has done. The Prince finds it in fragments and Maggie tells him that she knows of the situation between him and Charlotte.

It is precisely here, at the critical moment which has been led up to with infinite care and patience, that James shows his originality and his genius. Up till now, the interest of the situation has been more in the manner of treatment, in the fine shades of distinction drawn between imagination and fact, than in its intrinsic importance. For the situation *per se* is of course one that is very familiar. It could be handled in the mood of comedy—and one can imagine how a dramatist of the Restoration period would have dealt with it—or in the mood of tragedy. James does neither. In a sense his interest lies in the social comedy, using the word in its Meredithian connotation; but he is more vitally concerned with the response of character, with the civilized and completely conscious reaction to the full situation. I should like to emphasize these words—civilized and completely conscious.

In the first place, civilized. Life goes on; there is no passionate Othello-like reaction. Maggie and the Prince know; Charlotte suspects that Maggie knows; Maggie suspects that her father knows. Nothing is definitely said. The situation is apparently to go on, without comment and without reproach on either side. Maggie suffers, because for her the world is wrecked by her discovery, but she suffers in silence. One evening at their country-house she paces the terrace outside while the others play bridge indoors:

> She continued to walk and continued to pause; she stopped afresh for the look into the smoking-room, and by this time . . . she saw as in a picture . . . why it was she had been able to give herself so little, from the first, to the vulgar heat of her wrong. She might fairly as she watched them, have missed it as a lost thing; have yearned for it, for the straight vindictive view, the rights of resentment, the rages of jealousy, the tempests of passion, as for something she had been cheated of not least; a range of feelings which for many women would have meant so much, but which for *her* husband's wife, for *her* father's daughter figured nothing nearer to experience than a wild eastern caravan, looming into view with crude colours in the sun, fierce pipes in the air, high spears against the sky, all a thrill, a natural joy to mingle with, but turning off short before it reached her and plunging into other defiles. . . . It was extraordinary, they (the group playing inside) positively brought home to her that to feel about them in any of the immediate, inevitable, assuaging ways, the ways usually open to innocence outraged and generosity betrayed, would have been to give them up, and that giving them up, was, marvellously, not to be thought of.

It is just here that James shows his originality—his characters behave not in the way that one expects they would in a heightened situation—that is to say, there seems to be no impulsive, instinctive, and above all, no *violent* reaction. But they do behave as perfectly civilized people really would. Their responses are controlled all the time by the mind, it is true—James does not show us what happens when the mind is not so controlled. But, and equally importantly, the emotion *is* controlled—that is, it does exist and to a great degree. Maggie deliberately controls her feelings, refuses to act on impulse, for fear of disturbing the tremulous and delicate situation too roughly. She will not allow herself to succumb to her love for Amerigo because of her complete awareness that to do so would be to falsify the situation; that the only method of attaining any right issue is to stand back, not to interfere, in fact, to sacrifice.

In *The Sense of the Past* (to digress for a little), one of the two unfinished novels which James wrote, his last work, in 1915, there is a sentence which might stand as a motto for his work, and which throws more light on the connection between feeling and intellect in the novels. Ralph Pendrel, a young American who comes to Europe with a deep sense of its traditions, finds himself (it is a fantastic symbolic situation) actually taking the part of one of his ancestors and living in the past, with a group of people who take him to belong to their own time, while he is conscious both of their pastness, his contemporaneity with them, and at the same time his own modernity. He is involved in a queer situation, for his interlocutors appear to recognize that there is something strange about him in spite of his apparent conformity, and he realizes that the end will probably be disastrous—he faces this because, as James puts it, "he had come . . . out for nothing singly and solely . . . (but) the whole, the finest integrity of the thing."

The book is unfinished; it is indeed practically only begun; but in the notes Henry James has given us a full indication of how it was to be worked out. Nan Midmore, the daughter of the house in the past into which Ralph has stumbled, falls in love with him and he with her. Ultimately the question of Ralph's escape back into his own world, the modern world, rests on Nan's giving him up. On this Henry James obviously meant the whole plot to turn. "It is necessary," he says in the notes, where he is thinking out the novel (and anyone interested in his method of putting the novel together cannot do better than study the notes both in this and in the other novels), "it is necessary that she shall know (Ralph's situation) . . . in order to . . . do the particular thing that *will* act for him (*i.e.* to assist and relieve him), and so bring the whole situation to the point of its dénouement. What is then this particular thing? . . . *The* thing is to keep hold of the clue, as tight as possible, that I have grabbed for my solution in the line of her *making* the sacrifice—making it all with a sublime intelligence *for* him. . . . Isn't there something, isn't there even much, in the idea that when these two have arrived, so to speak, at their understanding . . . he becomes capable of a sort of sublimity in her presence . . . so that there is a kind of struggle between them as to who shall give up most—if I may put it in such a way without excess of the kind of romanticism that I don't want. . . . What hovers before me at this pitch, as I just said, is the "concetto" that, sincerely affected by her sublimity, he is moved to match it—and in all sincerity as I say—by offering to remain with her, as who should say, give up everything *for* her—from the moment he thus takes in that she gives him up for what is to herself utterly nothing, nothing but the exaltation of sacrifice."

The notion of renunciation here is plain enough. What I want now to stress is the phrase "without excess of the kind of romanticism I don't want." The danger Henry James has to avoid, in his last novel as in his first, is not that of dryness, of aridity, but of romantic excess, of sentimentality. His method, his technique helps him to avoid that—as he says when talking about working out the Ralph Pendrel situation: "Here the very closest and finest logic must govern all one's sequences." He avoids the danger of reading too much emotion into the situation, perhaps (his detractors will say) by reading too much *awareness* into the situation. But my point is that to react against romantic feeling in this way is very different from a complete absence of such feeling.

Let us now return to Maggie Verver, whom we left—in order to vindicate the charge of lack of feeling in the Jamesian character—passively contemplating the ruin of her happiness. As the situation develops, there is an extraordinarily delicate balancing of motive. Charlotte, who suspects that Maggie is aware of what has passed between Amerigo and herself but who does not know positively, boldly asks her if she has offended in any way for she has noticed a slight constraint. Maggie instead of telling her the truth positively denies it. James makes it amply clear why she lies, and this is extremely important —*if* Charlotte does not know that Maggie knows, then that can only mean that Amerigo has not told Charlotte of the final development of the situation; that is to say, the primary position has been reversed—instead of acting a part to Maggie while being completely in Charlotte's confidence, he is now acting a part to Charlotte in respect of a confidence which he and his wife share—the situation, as it were, follows with a logical consistency of emotion. To quote:

> "He must have had his own difficulty about it" (reasons Maggie), and she was not, after all, falling below him. . . . He had given her something to conform to, and she hadn't unintelligently turned on him, "gone back on him," as he would have said, by not conforming. They were together, he and she, close, close together—whereas Charlotte, though rising there radiantly before her, was really off in some darkness of space that would steep her in solitude and harass her with care. The heart of the Princess swelled, accordingly, even in her abasement; she had kept in tune with the right, and something, certainly, something that might be like a rare flower snatched from an impossible ledge, would, and possibly soon, come of it for her. The right, the right—yes, it took this extraordinary form of her humbugging, as she had called it, to the end. It was only a question of not, by a hair's-breadth, deflecting into the truth.

An astonishing statement, but one that is implied, if never stated again so clearly, in numerous instances. The situation in *The Wings of the Dove*, for instance, between Kate Croy, Milly Theale, and Merton Densher, is a fairly parallel one, where Milly Theale's reaction to her circumstance might be compared with Maggie's. Emphatically again the same attitude is taken in *What Maisie Knew*, a book where James' interest in form is perhaps at its height—each moment in the tale is logically progressive from the preceding one, and it moves forward with the utmost precision and economy. There is an extraordinarily skilful pattern of successive relationships, which could be represented as successive stages in the manipulation of a set of algebraic equations. There is, as it were, an increasing complexity of brackets within brackets, but behind the almost impossible intricacy, there lies concealed a solution in terms of a single constant. In this tale, where one is tempted at first sight to say that the interest is almost solely in the intricacies of pattern, what emerges—and emerges with triumphant force—is again this queer kind of Jamesian integrity, which depends on renunciation. This integrity is very rarely, in the novels, concerned with literal truth of fact or statement, and never concerned with ordinary conventional values. The Jamesian character is not interested in literal truth; but in a kind of absolute value, a value which can only be arrived at by a full and clear intelligence of everything involved. *Renunciation*, *integrity*, *awareness* are the three key-words for Henry James' work, and all are closely linked together.

In *The Golden Bowl*, for example, Maggie's passivity of action and silence makes her a force to be reckoned with, an admirable force. We are left at the end with no doubt as to the Prince's feeling for his wife; we are left with a hopeful remark about Adam's for Charlotte. The situation, as James might have said, has ended beautifully—it has been like an involved arrangement of pieces of a puzzle, and when the right pieces are put together, what happens? Well, nothing but the most admirable readjustment happens, provided everyone keeps his integrity. That of course is of the highest importance. There is nothing more striking than James' insistence that the responsibility for the individual's fate lies with the individual. Each man must act according to his own way.

Maggie's silence shows this, as much as it does her generosity. Charlotte will act according to her own laws; all Maggie can do is to help her do this.

The Golden Bowl indeed shows James' prepossessions with extreme clarity. On the one hand Maggie and Adam, dis-interested, un-selfish, *integer* characters; on the other the Prince and Charlotte. Each pair has a certain nobility—that is where the subtle discrimination of James' art, the finesse of his touch, is seen. In the case of the father and daughter the nobility manifests itself negatively, in sacrifice. On the other hand Charlotte and the Prince have a certain active beauty, which James recognizes to the full. The Prince however also knows the value of sacrifice—he does not withdraw from Charlotte but holds in loyalty to that relation; he does not, in other words, sacrifice her to himself. It is curious that the three who know what sacrifice is, should be those to attain harmony, and that Charlotte's great moment comes when she too resolutely accepts *her* sacrifice, and withdraws with Adam.

And now finally to indicate how *awareness* is essentially bound up with this notion of integrity. In the notes to *The Ivory Tower*, his last and unfinished work, and one which perhaps brings out the point most clearly, though all the novels do both implicitly and expressly, in the notes, James, talking of his principal character Gray Fielder, says:

> All of this makes him, I of course desperately realize, another of the "intelligent," another exposed and assaulted, active and "passive" mind, engaged in an adventure, and interesting in *itself* by so being; but I rejoice in that aspect of my material as dramatically and determinantly *general.*

It isn't *centrally* a drama of fools and vulgarians; it's only circumferentially and surroundedly so.

Another of the *intelligent*, another *exposed* and *assaulted* mind. Significant words. To what is Gray Fielder exposed and assaulted? He is a young man who falls heir to an immense fortune in America, a fortune amassed by an uncle who has been interested in nothing in his life except material gain, and who deliberately makes his nephew his sole heir because Gray is *not* so interested, because his values are the inner values of integrity. Gray's friend Rosanna Gaw (James' names are always odd) has been left a fortune by her narrow-minded rather unpleasant parent. Gray and Rosanna are the people who are aware that there is something more in the world than grab, than personal gratification. On the other hand are Horton Vint and Cissy Foy who are grasping, scheming, self-interested. Both have designs on their friends Gray and Rosanna. Horton wants to marry Rosanna, Cissy, Gray, in order to gain for themselves the advantages of wealth—to gain for themselves and each other, for Horton and Cissy are in love (The resemblance to the Charlotte—Amerigo—Maggie situation is plain). One of the most interesting and characteristic passages in the book occurs where Horton and Cissy discuss the possibilities of Cissy's marrying Gray:

> "There's one thing at any rate I'll be hanged if I shall allow," he wound up. . . . "He shan't become if I can help it as beastly vulgar as the rest of us."
>
> The thing was said with a fine sincere ring, but it drew from Cissy a kind of quick wail of pain. "Oh, oh, oh—what a monstrous idea . . . that he possibly *could*, ever!"

It had an immediate, even a remarkable effect; it made him turn at once to look at her, giving his lightest pleasantest laugh. . . . Then it made him, with a change of posture, shift his seat sufficiently nearer to her to put his arm round her altogether and hold her close, pressing his cheek a moment, with due precautions, against her hair. "That's awfully nice of you. We *will* pull something off. Is what you're thinking of what your friend out there *dans le temps*, the stepfather, Mr. Wendover, was it? told you about him in that grand manner?"

"Of course it is," said Cissy in lucid surrender and as if this truth were of a flatness almost to blush for. "Don't you know I fell so in love with Mr. Northover, whose name you mispronounce, that I've kept true to him for ever, and haven't been really in love with you in the least, and shall never be with Gray himself, however much I may want to, or you perhaps may even try to make me?—any more than I shall ever be with anyone else! . . ."

"I see, I see." It made Horton, for reasons, hold her but the closer—yet not withal as if prompted by her remarks to affectionate levity. It was a sign of the intercourse of this pair that, move each other as they might to further affection, and therewith on occasion to a congruous gaiety, they treated no cause and no effect of that sort as waste; they had somehow already so worked off, in their common interest, all possible mistakes and vain imaginings, all false starts and false pursuits, all failures of unanimity. "Why then if he's really so decent, not to say so superior," (Horton) went on, "won't it be the best thing in the world and a great simplification for you to fall—that is for you to *be*—in love with him? That will be better for me, you know, than if you're not; for it's the impression evidently made on you by the late Northover that keeps disturbing my peace of mind. I feel, though I can't quite tell you why," he explained, "that I'm never going to be in the least jealous of Gray and probably not even so much as envious; so there's your chance—take advantage of it all the way. Like him at your ease, my dear, and God send he shall like you! Only be sure it's for himself you do it—and for your own self; as you make out your possibilities, *de part et d'autre*, on your getting nearer to them."

"So as to be sure, you mean," Cissy enquired, "of not liking him for his money?"

He waited a moment, and if she had not immediately after her words sighed, "Oh dear, oh dear!" in quite another, that is a much more serious, key, the appearance would perhaps have been that for once in a blue moon she had put into his mind a thought he couldn't have. He couldn't have the thought that it was of the least importance she should guard herself in the way mentioned; and it was in the air, the very next thing, that she couldn't so idiotically have strayed as to mean to impute it. He quickly enough made the point that . . . The late Northover had clearly had something about him that it worried a fellow to have her perpetually rake up. *There* she was in peril of jealousy—his jealousy of the queer Northover ghost. . . . He could look after her with Gray—they were at one about Gray; what would truly alienate them, should she persist, would be his own exposure to comparison with the memory of a rococo Briton he had no arms to combat. Which extravagance of fancy had of course after a minute sufficiently testified to the clearance of their common air that invariably sprang from their feeling themselves again together and finding once more what this came to—all under sublime capability of proof. The renewed consciousness did perhaps nothing for their difficulties as such, but it did everything for the interest, the amusement, the immediate inspiration of their facing them: there was in that such an element of their facing each other and knowing, each time as if they had not known it before, that this had absolute beauty.

The interest of that passage lies in two things—in the

first place, it emphasizes the awareness which James wishes to stress; they rely for complete understanding on what is *not* said, taking the "beautiful intelligence" of each other for granted, so much so that here what they *mean* is actually the reverse of what they *say*; but no mistake is made by either as to their purpose. Secondly, it brings out the fact that the conflict between the two pairs of characters, between Horton and Cissy on the one hand, and Gray and Rosanna on the other, is not one crudely between good and evil, but between extremely finely organized intelligence with no sense of integrity, and extremely finely organized intelligence plus a sense of integrity. It is almost a duel of wits (and this is merely to point to a remarkably clear statement of what happens in all the novels).

In this case the plot centres (or would have centred, if finished) round the fact that Horton who acts as steward of Gray's money, defrauds him of it, and Gray, in accordance with the Jamesian tradition, knows that he does so, but takes no action, in fact ignores it. James' own remarks on this are illuminating:

> When the first definite question begins to glimmer upon Gray . . . as to what Horton is really doing with him, and as to whether or no he shall really try to find out. That question of whether or no he *shall* becomes the question. . . . The process of confrontation, reflection, resolution that ensues (on his knowledge), it is this that brings me up to my high point of beautiful difficulty and clarity.

And the "high point" is further explained:

> The way in which the standing off from sharp or supreme clearances is, and confirms itself as being, a note of my hero's

action in the matter. . . . No end, I think, to be got out of this wondrous fact of Gray's sparing Horton, or saving him, the putting of anything to a real or direct test.

This attitude of course is comparable to Maggie's in *The Golden Bowl*, to Strether's in *The Ambassadors*, to Milly Theale's in *The Wings of the Dove*. The end, although the tale is unfinished, is of course inevitable. Gray will triumph, as in their different ways, Maggie, Strether, Milly Theale triumph. At first sight, this may look like a concession to sentiment on James' part. Actually it isn't so. It is a curious kind of *negative* triumph—but none the less real. "Not, out of the whole affair, to have got anything for myself," says Strether. Continually, as Theodora Bosanquet well says of him, continually, in life, "wherever he looked he saw fineness apparently sacrificed to grossness, beauty to avarice, truth to a bold front; in the novels too, fineness is apparently sacrificed to grossness, beauty to avarice, truth to a bold front." But that is only half the question. The ultimate value, he knew, was not in the appearance, and out of *intelligent* sacrifice, emerges integrity, harmony, rightness. Intelligence is necessary. In a note to *The Ivory Tower*, James talks about the interest of the situation between Gray and Cissy—"the fascination," he calls it, "of the state of vigilance, the wavering equilibrium, at work." An extraordinarily interesting phrase, anticipating, in another field, Dr. Richards' remarks on "vigilance" in criticism.

Let me remind you of them. In *Principles of Literary Criticism*, he says:

In a high state of vigilance the nervous system reacts to stimuli with highly adapted, discriminating and ordered

> responses; in a lowered state of vigilance the responses are less discriminating, less delicately adapted.

(that is to say the poet is as it were more discriminating than others)—to continue:

> The answer then, at least in part, to the problem of how the poet's experience is more than usually available to him is that it is, as he undergoes it, more than usually organized through his more than usual vigilance.

It seems to me that this statement applies perfectly to James' work. Translate these terms from the critical to the moral world, and the reason is found for the value of James' characters. They show, with regard to moral problems, *i.e.* to problems of behaviour, a state of extreme vigilance, in which the best response, the response of the Strethers, the Milly Theales, the Grays, the Maggie Ververs, depends ultimately on a *fuller* state of consciousness than those of the Charlottes, the Hortons, the Kate Croys, admirable in many respects as these are. The best responses then, are the most delicately and fully organized. "Look at the situation, be aware, *see*," we might take Henry James to say; "and when you have done so, stand aside; your seeing it will bring out its full complexity." All his novels repeat this. "Don't grab, stand aside, and especially *see*," with emphasis particularly on the last word. And for his attitude and his individual way of dealing with it, I think we may fairly claim him, not only as a modern, but also as a writer of the most permanent and significant interest.

VIRGINIA WOOLF

In *A Room of One's Own*, an essay printed as the result of two lectures given, one at Girton College, one at Newnham College, Virginia Woolf says that the reason why women do not write is because they have not got £500 a year and a room of their own to write in. Whatever one may think of that statement, and it seems open to question if not to refutation, she herself is a writer who has opened up an entire new field for the novel. Later in the same book she deals with her main question, that of women's place in the literary world, and utters these significant words:

> Lamb, Browne, Thackeray . . . never helped a woman yet, though she may have learnt a few tricks of them and adapted them to her use. The weight, the pace, the stride of a man's mind are too unlike her own for her to lift anything substantial from him successfully. . . . Perhaps the first thing she would find, setting pen to paper, was that there was no common sentence ready for her use. All the great novelists like Thackeray and Dickens and Balzac have written a natural prose, swift but not slovenly, expressive but not precious, taking their own tint without ceasing to be common property. They have based it on the sentence that was current at the time. . . . It was a sentence that was unsuited for a woman's use.

She herself exemplifies how that sentence has been shaped.

To anyone who studies her works the question of style must be extremely important, style and technique—and that is what I propose to examine first.

The first two novels, *The Voyage Out* and *Night and Day* are curiously unlike the others in this respect. In *Night and Day* people and events are shown progressively with a fairly apparent logical connection between each successive happening. The movement is one along a straight line. Its main concern is the exposition of the situation between Katherine and Ralph Denham, that is to say the reconciling of different personalities into the unity of love. This is what Lawrence in his own way and by very different means expresses in his central book *Women in Love*. In Virginia Woolf the problem is considered by means of a very delicate analysis of mental states, something much more complicated and intricate than the physical basis with which Lawrence begins. The description of Katherine's feelings towards Denham is unequalled in her work, in its accurate, unromantic and most moving truth, except by the same theme in *The Voyage Out* where Rachel's bewildered feelings are analysed with the same delicacy and the same power.

This analysis then marks Virginia Woolf's first interest, but after all not an uncommon interest for a novelist—a novelist who in this respect derives from Stendhal and Henry James—to have. The unusualness of the presentation lies solely in the direct honesty to actual experience and the minute attention given to it; there is no trace of romantic convention but an almost scientific recording of each mood as it comes.

In *The Voyage Out*, which is indeed earlier in date than *Night and Day*, we have the first glimpse of Virginia Woolf's very characteristic method of attack. It occurs when one of the characters, Mrs. Ambrose, is walking down the London Embankment. We do not as yet know anything about Mrs. Ambrose—these are the first sentences which bring her to our notice:

> Someone is always looking into the river near Waterloo Bridge. . . . It is always worth while to look down and see what is happening. But this lady looked neither up nor down; the only thing she had seen, since she stood there, was a circular irridescent patch slowly floating past with a straw in the middle of it. The straw and the patch swam again and again behind the tremulous medium of a great welling tear, and the tear rose and fell and dropped into the river.

We are given a pictorial account of Mrs. Ambrose weeping, but we are not told why until some time later:

> She (wiped) . . . her eyes and (raised) them to the level of the factory chimneys on the other bank. She saw also the arches of Waterloo Bridge and the carts moving across them, like the line of animals in a shooting gallery. They were seen blankly, but to see anything was of course to end her weeping and begin to walk. . . . The fixity of her mood was broken by the action of walking. The shooting motor cars, more like spiders in the moon than terrestrial objects, the thundering drays, the jingling hansoms, and little black broughams, made her think of the world she lived in. Somewhere up there above the pinnacles where the smoke rose in a pointed hill her children were now asking for her and getting a soothing reply. . . .

This is a method of suggestive description which obviously affords considerable opportunities. We see first mistily through the quivering round tear the water which for her trembles through it, the embankment where she is standing, the house—in imagination—which she has just left, and the children there . . . ah, *that* is why she is crying!

See first, *connect* afterwards, says the artist. One seems continually to receive a stream of impressions which force themselves upon the attention at every moment of consciousness—what if the novelist, instead of selecting a few of these, as he had done in the past, should try to give some idea of their complexity? This is what Virginia Woolf herself states to be the problem of the novel, in one of the essays in *The Common Reader*:

> Examine for a moment an ordinary mind on an ordinary day. The mind receives a myriad impressions—trivial, fantastic, evanescent, or engraved with the sharpness of steel. From all sides they come, an incessant shower of innumerable atoms; and as they fall, as they shape themselves into the life of Monday or Tuesday the accent falls differently from of old; the moment of importance came not here but there; so that if a writer were a free man and not a slave, if he could write what he chose not what he must, if he could base his work upon his own feeling and not upon convention, there would be no plot, no comedy, no tragedy, no love interest or catastrophe in the accepted style and perhaps not a single button sewn on as the Bond Street tailors would have it. . . . Let us record the atoms as they fall upon the mind in the order in which they fall, let us trace the pattern, however disconnected and incoherent in appearance, which each sight or incident scores upon the consciousness. Let us not take it for granted that life exists more fully in what is commonly thought big than in what is commonly thought small.

The essay called *The Mark on the Wall* is a practical exposition of this technique, which has already been illustrated in the passage about Mrs. Ambrose (p. 3). At this point perhaps I should say that so far the technique is the same in both instances—the revelation of the "falling atoms" on the mind of a single person. Mrs. Ambrose in this respect may be considered as a projected form of the author's consciousness, whereas in *The Mark on the Wall* Virginia Woolf is concerned more directly with her own immediate associations. She starts off by seeing a small mark on the wall, and wonders what it can be:

> In certain lights, that mark on the wall seems actually to project from the wall. Nor is it entirely circular. I cannot be sure, but it seems to cast a perceptible shadow, suggesting that if I ran my finger down that strip of the wall it would, at a certain point, mount and descend a small tumulus, a smooth tumulus like those barrows on the South Downs which are, they say, either tombs or camps. Of the two I should prefer them to be tombs, desiring melancholy like most English people and finding it natural at the end of a walk to think of the bones stretched beneath the turf. . . .

This method of using the object as a point of departure is carried through the entire essay:

> There's no harm in putting a full stop to one's disagreeable thoughts by looking at a mark on the wall.
>
> Indeed, now that I have fixed my eyes upon it, I feel I have grasped a plank in the sea. . . . Here is something definite, something real. . . . Wood is a pleasant thing to think about. It comes from a tree; and trees grow, and we don't know how they grow. For years and years they grow, without paying any attention to us, in meadows, in forests and by the side of rivers—all things one likes to think about. The cows swish their tails beneath them on

> hot afternoons; they paint rivers so green that when a moorhen dives one expects to see its feathers all green when it comes up again. I like to think of the fish balanced against the stream like flags blown out; and of water-beetles slowly raising domes of mud upon the bed of the river. I like to think of the tree itself; first the close dry sensation of being wood; then there is the grinding of the storm; then the slow, delicious ooze of sap. I like to think of it, too, on winter's nights standing in the empty field with all leaves close-furled, nothing tender exposed to the iron bullets of the moon, a naked mast upon an earth that goes tumbling, tumbling, all night long. The song of birds must sound very loud and strange in June; and how cold the feet of insects must feel upon it, as they make laborious progresses up the creases of the bark, and sun themselves upon the thin green awning of the leaves, and look straight in front of them with huge diamond-cut red eyes.

There one can fairly clearly see the actual process in motion, and gathering momentum as it goes. The end of the essay gives the converse process of coming back to the object from which one has started, and conveys an excellent impression of the feeling both of haziness and of effort with which one comes back to actuality from, say, sleep or a hypnotic trance:

> It is full of peaceful thoughts, happy thoughts, this tree. I should like to take each one separately—but something is getting in the way. . . . Where was I? What has it all been about? A tree? A river? The Downs, Whitaker's *Almanack*, the fields of asphodel? I can't remember a thing. Everything's moving, falling, slipping, vanishing. . . . There is a vast upheaval of matter. Someone is standing over me and saying—
>
> "I'm going out to buy a newspaper."
>
> "Yes?"
>
> "Though it's no good, buying newspapers. Nothing

ever happens. . . . All the same, I don't see why we should have a snail on our wall."

Ah, the mark on the wall! It was a snail.

Nothing could be clearer than this demonstration, nor, within its limits, more artistically finished. Fix the object (which is here used as a bright flashing thing is used in some hypnotic experiments, and for the same effect—to enable the mind, while having an outward focus of attention, to retreat into the subconscious stream) and let the mind sway round all the associations it brings with the freedom and suppleness of a gymnast. It implies a very delicate balancing of attention—on the one hand sensitiveness to the subconscious free movement of thought or emotion, and on the other, a continual intellectual control.

The method of association is of course familiar to all of us who take the trouble to examine our mental experience at all, and it is especially used in poetry—the poetic imagery of Keats or Shakespeare depends largely on the associative value the word carries (*e.g.* in *The Eve of St. Agnes*, to take an obvious example, Keats talks of the window *all diamonded with panes of quaint device*; where the effect largely depends on the associations general to "diamond"—the hardness, coldness and purity, and in this case, of course, the angular shape). The poet who comes nearest to *formulating* the process, however is, curiously, Wordsworth, who in an important passage in the *Prelude* talks about objects *collateral* with the object seen, which sink into his mind and as he says, are

doomed to sleep
Until maturer seasons called them forth
To impregnate and to elevate the mind.

Virginia Woolf consciously exploits the method which Wordsworth here and in other places describes as a subconscious process. As she uses it, the method is allied to the free association used in the modern process of psychoanalysis, with this difference, that in her work the subject and the controlling observer are one and the same person.

The credit of originating this method in the novel, however, does not belong to Virginia Woolf but to Proust, who must have very greatly influenced her work and in whom the same very delicate sensibility to impressions (a necessity for this sort of approach) is obvious. In his description of the art of the painter Elstir in the second volume of *A l'Ombre des Jeunes Filles en Fleur*,[1] Proust indicates the *raison d'être* of this method; and the passage is such an important one that it deserves quotation:

> J'y pouvais discerner que le charme de chacune (peinture) consistait en *une sorte de métamorphose des choses représentées*,[2] analogue à celle qu'en poésie on nomme métaphore. . . .
>
> Parfois à ma fenêtre, dans l'hôtel de Balbec, le matin quand Françoise défaisait les couvertures qui cachaient la lumière, le soir quand j'attendais le moment de partir avec Saint-Loup, il m'était arrivé grâce à un effet de soleil, de prendre une partie plus sombre de la mer pour une côte éloignée, ou de regarder avec joie une zone bleue et fluide sans savoir si elle appartenait à la mer ou au ciel. Bien vite mon *intelligence rétablissait entre les éléments la séparation que*

[1] Vol. 2, p. 123 ff. *Nouvelle Revue Française.*
[2] The italics are mine throughout the passage.

mon impression avait abolie. C'est ainsi qu'il m'arrivait à Paris, dans ma chambre, d'entendre une dispute, presqu'une émeute, jusqu'à ce que j'eusse rapporté à sa cause, par exemple une voiture dont le roulement approchait, ce bruit dont j'éliminais alors les vociférations aiguës et discordantes que mon oreille avait réellement entendues, mais que mon intelligence savait que des roues ne produisaient pas. Mais les rares moments ou l'on voit la nature telle qu'elle est, poétiquement, c'était de ceux-la qu'était faite l'œuvre d'Elstir. . . .

Depuis les débuts d'Elstir nous avons connu ce qu'on appelle "d'admirables" photographies de paysages et de villes. Si on cherche à préciser ce que les amateurs désignent dans ce cas par cette épithète, on verra qu'elle s'applique d'ordinaire à quelque image singulière d'une chose connue, image différente de celles que nous avons l'habitude de voir, singulière et pourtant vraie, et qui à cause de cela est pour nous doublement saisissante *parce qu'elle nous étonne, nous fait sortir de nos habitudes, et tout à la fois nous fait rentrer en nous-mêmes en nous rappelant une impression. . . . Or, l'effort d'Elstir de ne pas exposer les choses telles qu'il savait qu'elles étaient mais selon les illusions optiques dont notre vision première est faite*, l'avait précisement amené à mettre en lumière certaines de ces lois de perspective, plus frappante alors, car l'art était le premier à les dévoiler. . . .

L'effort qu'Elstir faisait pour se dépouiller en présence de la réalité de toutes les notions de son intelligence était d'autant plus admirable que cet homme qui, avant de peindre, se faisait ignorant, oubliait tout par probité, car ce qu'on sait n'est pas à soi, avait justement une intelligence exceptionellement cultivée.

[Proust is here talking about the painter whom he calls Elstir, but who is generally recognized to be Monet (of whom Cézanne said, "He is only an eye, but what an eye"). Some very interesting articles which are relevant in this connection are to be found in the *British Journal of Psychology*, vols. xxi and xxii, "Phenomenal Regression to the Real Object," by R. H. Thouless. Extracts from these, perhaps the most important to the general reader, are quoted by Herbert Read in his book *Art Now* (Faber and Faber, 1933, p. 98). Thouless points out one very interesting thing for our purpose. He says (*British Journal of Psychology*, vol. xxii, p. 27 ff.):

> The child learning to draw in accordance with the laws of perspective is being taught to draw a projection of the object he is looking at on the plane of the picture. . . . That the laws of perspective do correctly describe the ways in which shapes, sizes, relationships of lines, etc., must appear on such a plane projection cannot, of course, be denied. . . . Teachers of perspective are, however, often not content to make these legitimate claims for the laws of perspective. They are inclined to say that the laws of perspective are the laws of the ways in which we "see," and to suggest that . . . methods of measurement with ruler, etc., are devices for finding out how we "really" see things . . . (The child's) drawing response is, on the contrary, being reconditioned to the stimulus object instead of to the phenomenal object.
>
> Some artists, moreover, have departed very far from perspective drawing. I have found that certain of the post-impressionist painters drew inclined objects in ratios which were about those of the phenomenal shapes as measured in the above experiments. It seems probable, therefore, that these were actually drawing the phenomenal and not the perspective figure. . . . The prime object of representational drawing is, of course, neither to reproduce shapes and sizes as the artist sees them nor to reproduce them in accordance with the laws of perspective, but to draw them in such a way that the perception of the drawing produces the same

> perceptual response of shapes and sizes as would the perception of the physical objects. . . .
>
> The picture which attempts only to be a two-dimensional pattern . . . was the declared aim of some of the post-impressionist painters. Here clearly the representational aim would be best attained by the drawing of the phenomenal figure. This may explain why such painters as Matisse have drawn the phenomenal figure.

Herbert Read, in a discussion of Matisse in *Art Now*, talks of his "integral vision," and says, "Matisse's paintings have been compared, not unreasonably, with children's drawings. Because in both you have the same *pre-logical vision*,[1] the same delight of the innocent eye." This of course is what Proust says of Elstir's art, though for him it is sophisticated, not childish—*l'effort de ne pas exposer les choses telles qu'il savait qu'elles étaient mais selon les illusions optiques dont notre vision première est faite.*]

What Proust brilliantly states here to be the artist's concern—to obtain sensations or sense-perceptions without the inhibiting process of intellectual understanding, to free the senses from the restraint which convention or habit imposes on an impression; to "mistake" the darker horizon of the sea for a prolongation of the shore, to hear the sounds of a sharp quarrel before one's intelligence has sorted out the fact that it is caused by creaking wheels—Virginia Woolf achieves by a method analogous to the painter's, that of free association. The object is thus revealed with an exquisite freshness, as for the first time. And this, of course, is again the intellectual re-formation

[1] The italicizing is mine.

of what Wordsworth especially and other poets have felt [1]—that art should remove that

> custom (which) lies upon (one) with a weight
> Heavy as frost, and deep almost as life.

One might note in passing that the process of memory with which Proust is concerned all through his gigantic work (significantly called *A la Recherche du Temps Perdu*), is also one of Wordsworth's chief preoccupations.

To return to Virginia Woolf—nothing perhaps could better illustrate her technique than the opening pages of *Jacob's Room*, where the child's impressions of the sands—the rock-pool, the red-faced holiday-makers asleep, the sheep's skull—are given with seeming inconsequence and with the shock of a first encounter. Events are focussed with the same shifting brilliance and surprise as in a kaleidoscope. Or again in the sketch called *Monday or Tuesday*, a rather more pronounced attempt to indicate the multiplicity of impressions which go to make up any day, as a multiplicity of days go to make up life. As this is complete in itself and also somewhat cruder and more precious (and therefore more easily to be seen critically) than the later more artistic handling, it may be useful at this point to quote it in full:

> Lazy and indifferent, shaking space easily from his wings, knowing his way, the heron passes over the church beneath the sky. White and distant, absorbed in itself, endlessly the sky covers and uncovers, moves and remains. A lake?

[1] Compare especially Blake—*The Marriage of Heaven and Hell*:
If the doors of perception were cleansed everything would appear to man as it is, infinite.
Blake, too, has a "*pre-logical* vision."

Blot the shores of it out. A mountain? Oh perfect—the sun gold on its slopes. Down that falls. Ferns then or white feathers, for ever and ever.

Desiring truth, awaiting it, laboriously distilling a few words for ever desiring—(a cry starts to the left, another to the right. Wheels strike divergently. Omnibuses conglomerate in conflict)—for ever desiring truth—(the clock asseverates with twelve distinct strokes that it is midday; light sheds gold scales; children swarm)—for ever desiring truth. Red is the dome; cones hang on the trees, smoke trails from the chimneys; bark, shout, cry "Iron for sale" —and truth?

Radiating to a point men's feet and women's feet, black or gold-encrusted—(This foggy weather—Sugar? No thank you—The commonwealth of the future)—the firelight darting and making the room red, save for the black figures and their bright eyes, while outside a van discharges, Miss Thingummy drinks tea at her desk, and plate glass preserves fur coats——

Flaunted, leaf-light, drifting at corners, blown across the wheels silver-splashed, home or not home, gathered, scattered, squandered in separate scales, swept up, down, torn, sunk, assembled—and truth?

Now to recollect by the fireside on the white square of marble. From ivory depths words rising shed their blackness, blossom and penetrate. Fallen the book; in the flame, in the smoke, in the momentary sparks—or now voyaging, the marble squares pendant, minarets beneath and the Indian seas, while space rushes blue and stars glint—truth? or now, content with closeness?

Lazy and indifferent the heron returns; the sky veils her stars; then bares them.

It is obvious here that the method employed is an extraordinarily good one for revealing the *chance* illuminations, the momentary impressions which fill the mind—in this instance the mind is like a sensitive plate which receives the impressions and develops them all quite clearly and all at the same time. It is equally obvious that any other chance set of impressions would here do almost as well to convey the feeling of flux, of incongruity, of the drifting forms which obscure at the same time as they are part of, the reality after which one strives. Again, clearly, there are two chief points of development for this method; one, the insistence on the value of *momentary* impressions, and secondly, the attempt at a kind of relativity—the feeling of everything going on at one and the same time. It will be seen that these two things form the chief technical considerations for Virginia Woolf; and in *Orlando*, which is more of a *jeu d'esprit* than anything else, are given practical illustration.

The difficulties of course are many. In the first place, what is to be done when the thing to be revealed in all its significance is not one subjective impression, but the numerous emotional or mental processes which form part of other people's experience? How, indeed, is one to make a novel on this plan? A torch flung into dark water lights up a thick tangle of reeds swaying under the surface of the stream. Sometimes in Virginia Woolf's novels it appears as if the *movement* of the stream had been forgotten. *Jacob's Room*, the first novel in which this method was fully employed, suffers from this defect, that the minute particulars, flawless in themselves, do not build up a total significant impression. Each mental incident analysed—Jacob as a child playing on the sands, a tea-party in Cambridge and talk after Hall, sailing a boat off Cornwall, London, the War—they are all emotionally relevant in themselves, but each incident is not emotionally relevant to the whole effect. It is indeed extraordinarily difficult—even the novelist, however much he wishes to, cannot find room for every impression; and in *Jacob's Room* one feels that the impressions chosen are arbitrary. Each moment is exquisitely done, but there is no central *point de repère*. Shifting that remark of E. M. Forster's in *A Passage to India* to bear a critical implication, one might say, "Here everything exists, nothing has value"; or, to put it the other way round—Everything has value but there is no discrimination.

Jacob's Room, then, gives the impression of a delicate and intricate spider's web from which the middle, the critical centre of radiation, has been torn away. In other words, *Jacob's Room* inevitably raises two questions: (1) the question of the necessity of a formed background of belief for the artist to work on (and from this question in one form or another there seems no escape if one is dealing with the modern novel) and (2) the question whether the method of illuminating the moment, of indicating the "luminous halo" in life may not lead to a forcing and therefore a falsification of its significance, to a desperate overpitching of the emotional content; or, to put it in another way, whether one may not be in danger of substituting a purely arbitrary and private mysticism for the more generally recognized foundations.

I should like to deal with some of these points by considering *Mrs. Dalloway*, *To the Lighthouse*, and *The Waves*. *Mrs. Dalloway* represents the first complete triumph of technique—in its way it is very near perfection. In it Virginia Woolf is not so much at the mercy of urgent associations which clamour to be expressed at the expense of proportion. Behind the figure of Clarissa, who is the central point of radiation, the background is gradually filled in—the sounds and sights of her familiar London—the slow mellow booming of Big Ben, the crisp air of Bond Street on a fresh summer morning, the rustle of children in the parks, the good-humoured bustle of the town as the buses begin to swing up and the traffic becomes heavy. Richard Dalloway, Clarissa, Peter, move against this background; and because they are people with memories it shifts and changes momentarily with their swaying thoughts. Nowhere in her work is there a better example of the co-ordination of time and place than in this book. Within the twelve hours of a waking day and in the limits of London we have been shown, by their own physical movements in a confined space and their mental movements in a comparatively unlimited field, three full-length portraits and an agonizingly accurate and piercing analysis of the state of mind which borders on lunacy. The contrast between Clarissa's world and that of Septimus is not fortuitous. By it Virginia Woolf achieves the same kind of impression of relativity as had been strikingly outlined in *Jacob's Room* (Fanny Elmer, Clara Durrant, Florinda revealed successively in a series of illuminating flashes). People and occurrences at different levels touch each other slightly, as the ripple cast by a stone in water trembles into the arc of another, and is vaguely disturbed.

Perhaps one quotation will serve to bring out the striking way in which one event is made as it were to focus all that is going on outside it—an achievement in effect similar but more subtle than that attained by Katherine Mansfield in the most exquisite of her short stories. The passage comes when Mrs. Dalloway is sitting in her drawing-room delicately mending her frock for the party:

> Quiet descended upon her, calm, content, as her needle, drawing the silk smoothly to its gentle pause, collected the green folds together and attached them, very lightly, to the belt. So on a summer's day waves collect, overbalance and fall; collect and fall; and the whole world seems to be saying "that is all" more and more ponderously, until even the heart in the body which lies in the sun on the beach says too, that is all. Fear no more, says the heart, committing its burden to some sea, which sighs collectively for all sorrows, and renews, begins, collects, lets fall. And the body alone listens to the passing bee; the wave breaking; the dog barking, far away barking and barking.

The rhythm of life has somehow managed to creep into the rhythm of that passage.

The close of Mrs. Dalloway is a masterpiece of technical excellence, the final appearance of Clarissa to those who love her being almost a symbol of the reason for the book's existence. Yet, if one is to criticize it fully, *Mrs. Dalloway* is not Virginia Woolf's highest accomplishment nor her most important work. The reason for this is that there is in it (unconsciously as far as the author is concerned) an unresolved contradiction in values. The passages which are meant to have most importance are those dealing with Clarissa and her world. The parts about Septimus, one suspects, were put in almost purely for the sake of contrast—in order to throw up the brightness and sparkle of Mrs. Dalloway's world, and also of course to reveal the general truth that brightness and shadow are co-existent.

But by some curious and unintended process, the shadow of Septimus affects our attitude to the rest of the book, and finally makes us doubt the value of the other world so delicately displayed before us—in fact the charge against the non-Septimian parts of a book which contains Septimus, is that they are almost too well done for what they represent.

In *To the Lighthouse*, however, we come to what must be recognized as Virginia Woolf's best work—in technique it marks a more subtle and yet more precise control, and in matter an extraordinarily acute unfolding of the relations of the Ramsay household, which centres round Mrs. Ramsay as the characters in *Mrs. Dalloway*—with the exception of the Septimus group—centre round Clarissa. Mrs. Ramsay's perceptions of other people are given side by side with other people's fleeting perceptions of Mrs. Ramsay, and in this way not only are the characters outlined very delicately and yet firmly, but what Matthew Arnold would have called a "criticism of life" is indicated. A quotation from a central scene in the book—the account of a dinner-party at Mrs. Ramsay's, will indicate how skilfully the intricate elements are drawn together to form a perfectly clear and coherent pattern in the reader's mind:

> But what have I done with my life? thought Mrs. Ramsay, taking her place at the head of the table, and looking at all the plates making white circles on it. "William, sit by me," she said. "Lily," she said, wearily, "over there." . . . At the far end was her husband, sitting down, all in a heap, frowning. What at? She did not know. She did not mind. She could not understand how she had ever felt any emotion or any affection for him. She had a sense of being past everything, through everything, out of every-

thing, as she helped the soup, as if there was an eddy—there —and one could be in it, or one could be out of it, and she was out of it. It's all come to an end, she thought, while they came in one after another, Charles Tansley— "Sit there, please," she said—Augustus Carmichael—and sat down. And meanwhile she waited, passively, for someone to answer her, for something to happen. But this is not a thing, she thought, ladling out soup, that one says.

Raising her eyebrows at the discrepancy—that was what she was thinking, this was what she was doing—ladling out soup—she felt, more and more strongly, outside that eddy; or as if a shade had fallen, and, robbed of colour, she saw things truly. The room (she looked round it) was very shabby. There was no beauty anywhere. She forbore to look at Mr. Tansley. Nothing seemed to have merged. They all sat separate. And the whole of the effort of merging and flowing and creating rested on her. Again she felt, as a fact without hostility, the sterility of men for if she did not do it nobody would do it, and so, giving herself the little shake that one gives a watch that has stopped, the old familiar pulse began beating, as the watch begins ticking—one, two, three, one, two, three. And so on and so on, she repeated, listening to it, sheltering and fostering the still feeble pulse as one might guard a weak flame with a newspaper. And so then, she concluded, addressing herself by bending silently in his direction to William Bankes—poor man! who had no wife and children, and dined alone in lodgings except for tonight; and in pity for him, life being now strong enough to bear her on again, she began all this business, as a sailor not without weariness sees the wind fill his sail and yet hardly wants to be off again and thinks how, had the ship sunk, he would have whirled round and round and found rest on the floor of the sea.

"Did you find your letters? I told them to put them in the hall for you," she said to William Bankes.

Lily Briscoe watched her drifting into that strange no-man's land where to follow people is impossible and yet their going inflicts such a chill on those who watch them that they always try at least to follow them with their eyes as one follows a fading ship until the sails have sunk beneath the horizon.

How old she looks, how worn she looks, Lily thought, and how remote. Then when she turned to William Bankes, smiling, it was as if the ship had turned and the sun had struck its sails again, and Lily thought with some amusement because she was relieved, Why does she pity him? For that was the impression she gave, when she told him that his letters were in the hall. Poor William Bankes, she seemed to be saying, as if her own weariness had been partly pitying people, and the life in her, her resolve to live again, had been stirred by pity. And it was not true, Lily thought; it was one of those misjudgments of hers that seemed to be instinctive and to arise from some need of her own rather than of other people's. He was not in the least pitiable. He has his work, Lily said to herself. She remembered, all of a sudden as if she had found a treasure, that she too had her work. In a flash she saw her picture, and thought, Yes, I shall put the tree further in the middle; then I shall avoid that awkward space. That's what I shall do. That's what has been puzzling me. She took up the salt-cellar and put it down again on a flower in the pattern in the table-cloth, so as to remind herself to move the tree.

"It's odd that one scarcely gets anything worth having by post, yet one always wants one's letters," said Mr. Bankes.

What damned rot they talk, thought Charles Tansley, laying down his spoon precisely in the middle of his plate, which he had swept clean, as if, Lily thought (he sat opposite to her with his back to the window precisely in the middle of the view), he were determined to make sure of his meals.

I have quoted this passage at length because I wish to contrast it later with a passage from *The Waves* in order to show the danger to which this method is subject. At the moment, however, it is enough to point to the superb control manifested here.

There is, in a sense, no plot in *To the Lighthouse.* In *Mrs. Dalloway* events take place in one day and thus there is a certain limitation of possible references, although, as I have said, the possibilities are widened by the swaying thoughts of the characters backwards and forwards from past to present time. In *To the Lighthouse* the event on which the book is built up is practically non-existent. Mrs. Ramsay's small boy, when the house-party is in the Hebrides, wants to make an expedition to the lighthouse the next day, but is prevented; years afterwards, when his mother is dead, he and his father make a visit to the place, now of course with all the glamour associated with it removed. Such might be said to be the skeleton of the "plot" but one states it only to say how little it affects what the book is really about. It is in its way a "search for time past," and in the last part of the novel, through perfectly definite and concrete illustrations, Virginia Woolf manages to convey something of the sense of loss, of change, of frustration through the passing of time, which is so difficult to formulate, and which by the individual may be revealed by a sigh or a momentary physical pang. In other words she is here well within the province usually assigned to poetry, and one of her achievements is to convey the "bouquet" of a mood or a series of conflicting moods, without loss either of atmosphere or accuracy.

Further, in *To the Lighthouse*, Mrs. Ramsay is contrasted with Lily Briscoe the artist who never quite succeeds in putting her ideal picture on canvas, much as in *The Voyage Out* (which contains the germs of the later book and should be read in connection with it) Mrs. Ambrose is contrasted with Rachel. Mrs. Ambrose (who is a sort of first sketch of Mrs. Ramsay), and Mrs. Ramsay supply the practical complement to Rachel and Lily who represent the artist's view of life—Mrs. Ambrose and Mrs. Ramsay are the people who live, who manage to deal with life as though, miraculously, it were art and could be shaped and moulded.

Mrs. Ambrose is in this respect a shadow of what Mrs. Ramsay is to become. Yet though we see little of her, the account of her beauty, her kindness, her unconventionality, casts a statue-like shadow, and she is in some way significant. Why she should be so comes out if one compares a short and seeming trivial passage at the beginning of the book, with the recurring theme of *To the Lighthouse*. It occurs in the description of the first dinner-party with the Dalloways on board ship (the sharp thumb-nail sketch of the Dalloways relates *The Voyage Out* to *Mrs. Dalloway*—Clarissa remains constant in both, but how Richard has improved as he grows older. Can he possibly be the same person ?—that grave silent Richard who buys roses for his wife because he cannot tell her he loves her, and the fatuous, platitudinous politician of the earlier book ?) Richard speaks:

> "We politicians doubtless seem to you" (he grasped somehow that Helen (Mrs. Ambrose) was the representative of the arts) "a gross commonplace set of people; but we see both sides; we may be clumsy, but we do our best to get a grasp of things. Now your artists *find* things in a mess,

shrug their shoulders, turn aside to their visions—which I grant may be very beautiful—and *leave* things in a mess. . . ."

"It's dreadful," said Mrs. Dalloway. . . . "I should like to stop all the painting and writing and music until this kind of thing exists no longer. Don't you feel," she wound up, addressing Helen, "that life's a perpetual conflict?"

Helen considered a moment. "No," she said, "I don't think I do."

Helen does not feel the conflict; on the other hand, Mrs. Ramsay, in *To the Lighthouse* resolves it. She adjusts life and people with the same perfection and serenity and completion as Lily Briscoe tries to attain in art. The problem of life and of art is in fact the same—to make the moment perfect, to harmonize differences, to obtain a central significance. Mrs. Ambrose does not quite do this; Mrs. Ramsay does. Because she does, life flows through the book like light through a web, illuminating people and their relationships.

To Lily, Mrs. Ramsay resolved everything into simplicity; made these angers, irritations fall off like old rags; she brought together this and that and then this, and so made out of that miserable silliness and spite (she and Charles squabbling, sparring, had been silly and spiteful) something . . . which survived after all these years, complete, so that she dipped into it to refashion her memory of him and it stayed in the mind almost like a work of art.

"Like a work of art," she repeated. And . . . the old question which traversed the sky of the soul perpetually, the vast, the general question which was apt to particularize itself at such moments as these, when she released faculties that had been on the strain, stood over her, darkened over her. What is the meaning of life? That was all—a simple question; one that tended to close in on one with years.

The great revelation had never come. The great revelation perhaps never did come. Instead there were little daily miracles, illuminations, matches struck unexpectedly in the dark; here was one. This, that, and the other; herself and Charles Tansley and the breaking wave; Mrs. Ramsay bringing them together; Mrs. Ramsay saying "Life stand still here"; Mrs. Ramsay making of the moment something permanent (as in another sphere Lily herself tried to make of the moment something permanent) this was of the nature of a revelation. In the midst of chaos there was shape; this eternal passing and flowing (she looked at the clouds going and the leaves shaking) was struck into stability. Life stand still here, Mrs. Ramsay said. "Mrs. Ramsay! Mrs. Ramsay!" she repeated. She owed this revelation to her.

Further, in *To the Lighthouse* Virginia Woolf is saying quite clearly—just as in *The Mark on the Wall* she exposed her technique clearly—that life is the centre of art. One remembers that incident in *Jacob's Room* where Mrs. Flanders' black parasol supplies just the necessary touch to make Charles Steele's picture complete. In the dinner-party passage in *To the Lighthouse* (p. 53 above), the overflow of Mrs. Ramsay's mood affects Lily and Lily's picture. More explicitly, the book ends with a long passage the intention of which is quite unmistakeable. Lily is struggling with her refractory painting and thinking at the same time of Mrs. Ramsay and all she stood for (it is of course some time after Mrs. Ramsay's death):

> There was something perhaps wrong with the design? Was it, she wondered, that the line of the wall wanted breaking, was it that the mass of the trees was too heavy? She smiled ironically; for had she not thought, when she began, that she had solved her problem?

What was the problem then? She must try to get hold of something that evaded her. It evaded her when she thought of Mrs. Ramsay; it evaded her now when she thought of her picture. . . . But one got nothing by soliciting urgently. One got only a glare in the eye from looking at the line of the wall, or from thinking—she wore a grey hat. She was astonishingly beautiful. Let it come, she thought, if it will come. For there are moments when one can neither think nor feel.

. . . . . .

Suddenly the window at which she was looking was whitened by some light stuff behind it. At last then somebody had come into the drawing-room; somebody was sitting in the chair. For Heaven's sake, she prayed, let them sit still there and not come floundering out to talk to her. Mercifully whoever it was stayed still inside; had settled by some stroke of luck so as to throw an odd-shaped triangular shadow over the step. It altered the composition of the picture a little. It was interesting. It might be useful. Her mood was coming back to her. . . . One wanted, she thought, dipping her brush deliberately, to be on a level with ordinary experience, to feel simply that's a chair, that's a table, and yet at the same time, It's a miracle, it's an ecstasy. The problem might be solved after all. Ah, but what had happened? Some wave of white went over the window-pane. The air must have stirred some flounce in the room. Her heart leapt at her and seized her and tortured her.

"Mrs. Ramsay! Mrs. Ramsay!" she cried, feeling the old horror come back—to want and want and not to have. Could she inflict that still? And then, quietly, as if she refrained, that too became part of ordinary experience, was on a level with the chair, with the table. Mrs. Ramsay—it was part of her perfect goodness to Lily—sat there quite simply, in the chair, flicked her needles to and fro, knitted her reddish-brown stocking, cast her shadow on the step. There she sat.

. . . . .

She turned to her canvas. There it was—her picture. Yes, with all its green and blues, its lines running up and across, its attempt at something. It would be hung in the attics, she thought; it would be destroyed. But what did that matter? she asked herself, taking up her brush again. She looked at the steps; they were empty; she looked at her canvas; it was blurred. With a sudden intensity, as if she saw it clear for a second, she drew a line there, in the centre. It was done; it was finished. Yes, she thought, laying down her brush in extreme fatigue, I have had my vision.

The meaning of this is obvious—the imaginary apparition of Mrs. Ramsay to Lily expresses in symbol the fact that the artist must understand something of the art of living before he or she can make composition perfect.

In *To the Lighthouse* art and life are no longer hostile to each other; they both unite in their attempt to achieve perfection of the moment in differing material. In this book Virginia Woolf has expressed permanently something which she had attempted to express more or less partially in the earlier books. (*To the Lighthouse* supplies a clue to *Jacob's Room* and *Mrs. Dalloway* in their emphasis on the moment.) The theme which was recessive in *The Voyage Out* has now become dominant, and in the manner of expression not even *Orlando* that triumphant exercise in technique, not even *Jacob's Room* can surpass it. It is the distinctive excellence of *To the Lighthouse* that in it a critical and significant problem has been expressed in terms of character, and so, has been solved.

In *To the Lighthouse*, also, Virginia Woolf has brilliantly illustrated and justified the full resources of her technique, which by collecting the tenuous and momentary impressions floating into the mind manages to reveal as it were the solid reality which they together make up.

The Waves seems to me to be in very different case, and that in spite of the fact that technically it shows the extreme limit to which the method can go. Here the associative technique is used in order to give the impression of life as composed of multitudes of atoms dancing now in sunlight, now in darkness, with no apparent purpose or coherence. There is a good deal of what one might call subtle counter-pointing throughout. The successive chapters, which express in the form of lyrical monologue, the gradual development of individual consciousness, the several stages of the individual's existence, are extremely closely bound together—the cross-references to incident and sensation resemble phrases in music which mark the development of the theme (the comparison with Wagner is obvious). *Musically*, in Pater's sense, the book is flawless, and that in a way new to the novel. Plot has been practically abandoned, but the characters are clearly differentiated through their self-revelations. Each speaks in turn, and at the end Bernard, the artist, the phrase-maker, sums up his own life and theirs. In this book, Virginia Woolf is clearly giving a practical demonstration of what she had suggested in *The Common Reader*:

"Life is not a series of gig-lamps symmetrically arranged; life is a luminous halo, a semi-transparent envelope surrounding us from the beginning of consciousness to the end.

Is it not the task of the novelist to convey this varying, this unknown and circumscribed spirit, whatever aberration or complexity it may display, with as little mixture of the alien and external as possible?"

Further, the book is obviously an important document in contemporary literary history. Unmistakeably, here, a voice of the same age is speaking as that which is heard in *The Waste Land*, and there are Eliotian references throughout. When Bernard says:

> "For this is not one life; nor do I always know if I am man or woman, Bernard, or Neville, Louis, Susan, Jinny, or Rhoda—so strange is the contact of one with another"—

we are reminded of T. S. Eliot's *Tiresias*. The actual verbal reminiscence is at times striking; for example, the analogy between Bernard's:

> "Now the meal is finished; we are surrounded by peelings and breadcrumbs. . . . Is it Paris, is it London where we sit, or some Southern city of pink-washed houses lying under cypresses, under high mountains, where eagles soar?"

and the "Where are the eagles and the trumpets?" of *A Cooking Egg* is too close to be undeliberated. There is, too, something of the same juxtaposition of the trivial and the tragic, of beauty and horror, in this book as in *The Waste Land*.

Yet, somehow, the result is not entirely satisfactory. *The Waves* is a book which raises many questions, notably those asked in *To the Lighthouse*—What is life? What is art? An answer is indeed indicated in the last chapter, but with a strange distrust. More than any other, this novel makes one wonder whether, without "beliefs" of some kind the emotion in a work will not seem forced.

One cannot, of course, ask the poet or novelist for specific moral sanctions; the artist's concern, like the scientist's, is in the experience—here is the actual experience; this is what it is, he says, and need say no more. But art is always straying over into life, and *The Waves* raises ungrateful questions. It leaves one with a curious sense of barrenness, in spite of some exquisite moments. Why this should be so may come out by a comparison of the passage quoted from *To the Lighthouse* (on p. 53) with the passage at the end of *The Waves* where Bernard suddenly feels the meaninglessness of life and afterwards the renewal of it, both apparently from entirely arbitrary causes:

> Something always has to be done next. Tuesday follows Monday; Wednesday, Tuesday. Each spreads the same ripple. The being grows rings, like a tree. Like a tree, leaves fall.
>
> For one day as I leant over a gate that led into a field, the rhythm stopped; the rhymes and the humming, the nonsense and the poetry. A space was cleared in my mind. I saw through the thick leaves of habit. . . . I waited. I listened. Nothing came, nothing. I cried then with a sudden sense of complete desertion. Now there is nothing. No fin breaks the waste of this immeasurable sea. Life has destroyed me. . . .
>
> The scene beneath me withered. . . . The woods had vanished; the earth was a waste of shadow. No sound broke the silence of the wintry landscape. No cock crowed; no smoke rose; no train moved. A man without a self, I said. A heavy body leaning on a gate. A dead man. With dispassionate despair, with entire disillusionment, I surveyed the dust dance; my life, my friend's lives. . . . How can I proceed now, I said, without a self, weightless

and visionless, through a world weightless and without illusion?

. . . . .

How then does light return to the world after the eclipse of the sun? Miraculously. Frailly. In thin stripes. It hangs like a glass cage. It is a hoop to be fractured by a tiny jar. There is a spark there. Next moment a flush of dun. Then a vapour as if earth were breathing in and out, once, twice, for the first time. Then under the dullness someone walks with a green light. Then off twists a white wraith. The woods throb blue and green, and gradually the fields drink in red, gold, brown. Suddenly a river snatches a blue light. The earth absorbs colour like a sponge slowly drinking water. It puts on weight; rounds itself; hangs pendent; settles and swings beneath our feet.

So the landscape returned to me; so I saw fields rolling in waves of colour beneath me. . . . Loveliness returns as one looks, with all its train of phantom phrases. One breathes in and out substantial breath; down in the valley the train draws across the fields lop-eared with smoke.

Compare with this the dinner-party passage in *To the Lighthouse*, where a similar experience of sudden loss and sudden recovery of value is given. I think it is true to say that in *To the Lighthouse* the mood depends for its value on the human element of pity, sympathy, and so on. (Compare for the same sort of emphasis the account of Lily Briscoe's vision of Mrs. Ramsay.) Here the mood is almost completely arbitrary, and arises and dissipates for no particular reason. Wordsworth's miraculous little poem, "At the Corner of Wood Street," ends thus:

She looks and her heart is in Heaven; but they fade,
The mist and the river, the hill and the shade;
The stream will not flow, and the hill will not rise,
And the colours have all passed away from her eyes.

The effect of those lines, and especially of the last two where the feeling both of effort and of the slipping and vanishing of colour are given by the movement of the rhythm, is re-inforced by, if it does not ultimately depend on, the fact that it arises from the human basis of regret for something lovely or longed-for, vanished. In Virginia Woolf's exquisite description of the re-birth of colour there is no particular emotional justification as a *basis* for the experience. The experience as it were springs out of the air—it is a phenomenon of a momentary emotion, and interesting; but (to use a phrase of Eliot's perhaps already too much worn) it has no "tentacular roots" like the other has. The criticism which one applied to *Jacob's Room*, that there seemed to be no *complete* emotional validity in it, might also be applied to *The Waves*, in spite of the extremely sensitive and delicate understanding of particular moods revealed in it.

To sum up, in Virginia Woolf's work there is both an exceedingly delicate sensibility to impressions and a critical intelligence sufficiently in control to order the multiplicity of impressions into an artistic unity. The advantages of her subtle method is that it comes closer and closer to the actual experience; the danger is that it may, as I think it does in *The Waves*, cause the experience to assume more significance than it actually holds. There is also the danger of completion. For once this method is perfected, there only remains to record, and the record of any one person, however sensitive, must be limited to the consciousness of his consciousness.

The instrument of communication in this case is perfect. There only remains to decide whether in E. M.

Forster's phrase, "it is impossible for the instrument of contemplation to contemplate itself; perhaps if it is possible it means the end of imaginative literature," and secondly, what Virginia Woolf herself says in an essay:

> From what . . . arises that sense of security which gradually, delightfully, and completely overcomes us? It is the power of their belief—their conviction, that imposes itself upon us. In Wordsworth, the philosophic poet, this is obvious enough. But in both (Scott and Jane Austen) there is the same natural conviction that life is of a certain quality. They have their judgment of conduct. They know the relations of human beings towards each other and towards the universe. Neither of them probably has a word to say about the matter outright, but everything depends on it. Only believe, we find ourselves saying, and all the rest will come of itself. . . .
>
> So then our contemporaries afflict us because they have ceased to believe. The most sincere of them will only tell us what it is that happens to himself. . . . Set down at a fresh angle of the eternal prospect they can only whip out their notebooks and record with agonized intensity the flying gleams, which light on what? and the transitory splendours which may, perhaps, compose nothing whatever.

It is curious that Virginia Woolf, who exemplifies how far the instrument of contemplation can contemplate itself, should also raise, and raise very strongly, the second question.

E. M. FORSTER

If with Henry James one leaps from the 70's to the most complete modernism, with E. M. Forster one has at first at any rate to proceed backwards. Forster's early writings clearly owe a great deal to Meredith, although eventually he goes very far beyond the limits of the Meredithian theme. But the early influence is interesting to see, particularly because it helps to make clear the characteristic and individual attitude which emerges in the later novels.

Forster himself makes explicit reference to Meredith in *Aspects of the Novel*, the published version of lectures given a few years ago at Cambridge . . . "Meredith is not (now) the great name he was twenty or thirty years ago, when much of the Universe and all Cambridge trembled"—that is to say about the time when Forster's own first works (*Where Angels Fear to Tread* and *The Longest Journey*) were appearing. And he goes on, in a slightly derogatory way—"His philosophy has not worn well. His heavy attacks on sentimentality—they bore the present generation, which pursues the same quarry, but with neater instruments, and is apt to suspect anyone carrying a blunderbuss of being a sentimentalist himself." A neat statement; but the charge of sentimentality might equally be made against part of Forster's own work—in *The*

Longest Journey, for example; although certainly Forster in the main is of the modern generation in this respect, that he "pursues the same quarry, but with neater instruments."

In *A Room with a View* Forster makes an explicit reference to Meredith which it is impossible to ignore. Cecil Vyse, the staid and unimaginative fiancé of Lucy, brings to their corner of the world two people with whom Lucy has had an adventure in Italy, as a kind of practical joke, a joke which ironically turns on him. When he tells Lucy that the Emersons are coming, he says:

> I, even I, have won a great victory for the Comic Muse. George Meredith's right—the cause of Comedy and the cause of Truth are really the same.

Again, when old Mr. Emerson sets forth his views in reply to a casual remark made by one of the party of young people he meets when they are going to bathe:

> [1] "And yet you will tell me the sexes are equal?"
> "I tell you that they shall be," said Mr. Emerson, who had been slowly descending the stairs. "Good afternoon, Mr. Beebe. I tell you they shall be comrades. . . ."
> "We are to raise ladies to our level?" the clergyman enquired.
> "The garden of Eden," pursued Mr. Emerson, still descending, "which you place in the past, is really yet to come. We shall enter it when we no longer despise our bodies."
> Mr. Beebe disclaimed placing the Garden of Eden anywhere.
> "In this—not in other things—we men are ahead. We despise the body less than women do. But not until we are comrades shall we enter the garden."

[1] One should remember that this was written in 1909.

"I say, what about this bathe," murmured Freddy, appalled at the mass of philosophy that was approaching him.

"I believed in a return to Nature once. But how can we return to Nature when we have never been with her? Today, I believe that we must discover Nature. After many conquests we shall attain simplicity. It is our heritage."

In spite of the amusingly flippant tone, it is impossible not to feel that Forster is here in direct sympathy with Meredith's remark in the *Essay on Comedy*:

> There never will be civilization where Comedy is not possible, and that comes of some degree of social equality of the sexes . . . where women are on the road to an equal footing with men, in attainments and in liberty—in what they have won for themselves, and what has been granted them by a fair civilization—there . . . pure comedy flourishes.

Yet a third point of resemblance—and the most important—is in Forster's attitude to Nature. It comes out of course in the last part of the extract already quoted, and most of the short stories in the early collection *The Celestial Omnibus*, bring it out—for example *The Story of a Panic* or the one called *Other Kingdom*. In these he is not merely retelling a classical legend in a modern background. The tale of the boy who has been touched by Pan, the girl who vanishes into a wood to escape the possessive hand of the materialist, express in symbol something which underlies a great deal of Forster's work.

In a sense he is, like Meredith, a happy pagan, believing in the freedom and solid goodness of earth, of the natural life; but—and much more important—his paganism is definitely stressed as against other qualities which the civilized world possesses and which seem to be definitely inhibiting or destructive. In this he is perhaps as near D. H. Lawrence as Meredith, and D. H. Lawrence is a writer from whom Forster is not so far away as critics would have us believe.

The Story of the Siren (published in *The Eternal Moment*, a not very good collection of short stories, most of them open to the charge of sentimentality) brings out this point very clearly.

It is much the same kind of semi-supernatural tale as those that appear in the collection called *The Celestial Omnibus*; it is told as reported by an Italian peasant, a fisherman who recounts a legend of the coast. The sea, he says, is the home of a siren of incredible beauty, and some people who have dived deep have been lucky enough to see her. Thereafter they are good for nothing in the world, and are as though possessed—but possessed of some secret which makes ordinary life nonsensical. The fisherman's brother is one of those who had seen the siren, and who is thus transformed. He hears of a girl to whom the same thing has happened; they marry, are extremely happy; she is about to have a child. At this the superstitious villagers are alarmed. They think some great disaster will happen when the child of two such people is born. As the fisherman puts it:

> The siren will then rise from the sea, and destroy silence, and save the world.

The priest of the village, to whom all this belief in the siren is absurd, but at the same time frightening, meets the girl walking by the cliff-edge and causes her to stumble and fall into the sea to drown. That is all. But it gives occasion for two remarks in the course of the narrative which are significant for our purpose. The first comes when the fisherman curses the religion which seems to have caused all the misery:

> He cursed the priests, the lying filthy cheating immoral priests who had ruined his life. . . . "Thus are we tricked," was his cry, and he stood up and kicked at the azure ripples with his feet, till he had obscured them with a cloud of sand.

The second remark comes at the very end of the story, and is of the same kind. Forster has heard him and is ruminating on what he has heard:

> I heard him say, "Silence and loneliness cannot last for ever. It may be a hundred or a thousand years but the sea lasts longer, and she shall come out of it and sing." I would have asked him more, but at that moment the whole cave darkened, and there rode in through its narrow entrance the returning boat.

These are of course symbolical statements—"He kicked at the azure ripples with his feet, until he had obscured them with a cloud of sand"; "At that moment the whole cave darkened, and there rode in through its narrow entrance the returning boat"—it is Forster's method—a subtle one—of interposing a personal comment. The priests confuse the truth, the shining truth with their dusty dry beliefs; modern civilization darkens the pagan vision which might otherwise have been illuminating.

The same attitude comes out extremely clearly in *A Room with a View*, in some of old Mr. Emerson's remarks. Mr. Emerson is a childlike old man who has a few simple beliefs in beauty and kindness and who disregards or over-rides the conventions, filling the rooms of people whom he does not know with violets, insisting that the newcomers to the Italian pension shall have his room because it has a view, instead of their own which looks out on a blank wall—he is obviously a trouble to the conventionally minded. A clergyman in the Italian party has warned Lucy against him and says that he "practically murdered his wife in the sight of God." Later in the story Lucy meets Mr. Emerson when his son George is dangerously ill: He tells her that George "has gone under—as his mother did."

> "But Mr. Emerson . . . what are you talking about?"
> "When I wouldn't have George baptized," said he. Lucy was frightened.
> "And she agreed that baptism was nothing, but he caught that fever when he was twelve, and she turned round. She thought it a judgment." He shuddered. "Oh, horrible—worst of all—worse than death, when you have made a little clearing in the wilderness, planted your little garden, let in your sunlight, and then the weeds creep in again! A judgment! And our boy had typhoid because no clergyman had dropped water on him in church. Is it possible, Miss Honeychurch? . . . Shall we slip back into the darkness for ever?"
> "I don't know," gasped Lucy. "I don't understand this sort of thing. I was not meant to understand it."
> "But Mr. Eager [the clergyman who had told Lucy of the "murder"]—he came when I was out, and acted according to his principles. I don't blame him or anyone . . . but by the time George was well she was ill. He made her think about sin and she went under thinking about it."

It was thus that Mr. Emerson had murdered his wife in the sight of God.

"Oh, how terrible," said Lucy, forgetting her own affairs at last.

"He was not baptized," said the old man. "I did hold firm." And he looked with unwavering eyes at the rows of books, as if—at what cost!—he had won a victory over them. "My boy shall go back to the earth untouched."

There is no doubt that Forster means that paganism is valuable. The further question is, what does he mean by paganism? Is it a convenient name for something more intricate? And this is where one comes to Forster's own contribution to the novel. His attitude to comedy, to the necessity for equality (in the sense of companionship) between men and women, at first glance his attitude towards Nature—all seem Meredithian and derived. But Forster's own voice is heard unmistakeably developing the theme, and finally going a long way beyond anything that Meredith would have anticipated. This will be clearer if we examine the three early novels in some detail, before going on to a consideration of *Howard's End* and *A Passage to India*, where his attitude has become modified to a large extent.

I

An examination of *The Longest Journey* brings out Forster's point of view most clearly. The "story" is neither here nor there—it is a long leisurely somewhat unwieldy and shapeless plot where we follow the chief character Rickie from his undergraduate days at Cambridge—and Forster has caught the atmosphere of Cambridge better than anyone else has done, much better than

Virginia Woolf does in *Jacob's Room*—to his life as a master at a small private school, unhappy marriage, and sudden death while trying to save his half-brother Stephen from being killed by an oncoming train.

Stephen is an important character—he is rough, unintellectual, countrified. He is the illegitimate son of Rickie's mother; at first Rickie does not know of the relationship; when he does he is revolted, having cherished the memory of his mother as something infinitely pure and untouched; then he tries to be kind to Stephen for the sake of his mother's memory. Stephen, being robust emotionally, will not have this sham affection, and the book turns on the rehabilitation of Rickie's self-respect when he begins to like Stephen for himself. Stephen is obviously, in Forster's sense, pagan, with the pagan virtues of honesty and impulsive action; all that he does he does from his whole self, unsuppressed. One is asked to postulate here (as with Gino and George in the later books) that in Stephen we have evidence of "pure" feeling, in the chemical sense. It is a large assumption to make, especially as the characters as such are not very convincing, although they are obviously embodiments of an attitude which Forster feels to be very valuable. He is much happier with the group than with the individual—for example the superb description of the dining-room of the pension Bertolini in *A Room with a View*—and for this reason as a comic artist he is on sure ground. When he touches the borderline of tragedy, as in this case, one is just a little uncertain that the effect will not be melodramatic. However, the main concern of the book is symbolized in Rickie—he is represented as a person who at first is on the side of freedom, of intellectual and emotional honesty, who becomes involved in the conventional response, the conventional attitude, and is finally freed again through his meeting with Stephen.

As Rickie himself hovers between the two attitudes, the emphasis falls very clearly where Forster wants it—the contrast is continually stressed between the life of earth, the life of intuition and reality, represented by Stephen and Rickie's mother; and the life of convention, of sham values, represented by Pembroke the schoolmaster, Mrs. Failing, and Rickie's father. A very important point to notice is that Forster occasionally checks the romantic feeling induced by the first attitude, by a sort of acid sub-comment—for example the scene where Rickie, after he and Stephen have broken free from the Pembroke household, meditates peacefully in his aunt's drawing-room, secure in the consciousness of a new and free existence. He feels renewed through contact with Stephen's life of impulse—the earth is good, the earth is vital—"he knew that conventions are not majestic, and that they will not claim us in the end." As he muses thus, one of his aunt's priceless coffee-cups slips from his fingers and breaks in pieces on the floor. This is Forster's method of ironic comment on his enthusiasm. It is a favourite method of his to combine intellectual detachment with the mood of "inspiration" or belief, as though he distrusted the imaginative vision at the same time as he exhorts us to trust it.[1]

[1] A similar subtlety is seen in Mr. Myers' *The Root and the Flower*. One might take Forster and Myers as being symptomatic, in this respect, of their time.

Later in the book, Rickie, going in search of Stephen, finds that he has broken his promise and is roaring drunk, which means for Rickie the collapse of the fine world which they had meant to build up together:

> He leant against the parapet and prayed passionately, for he knew that the conventions would claim him soon. God was beyond them, but ah, how far beyond, and to be reached after what degradation . . . (His vision) meant nothing . . . they all meant nothing and were going nowhere, the whole affair was a ridiculous dream.

Believing this, he saves Stephen in his drunkenness from the oncoming train, and is killed himself. His last words imply a complete revulsion from his narrowly gained standards of freedom, to all that he had previously thought valueless, they are an admission of defeat.

The book, however, does not end there. The life of earth in Stephen emerges triumphant by reason of Rickie's act. We are left with Stephen in complete harmony with life, remembering Rickie with gratitude and love:

> He had always been grateful, as people who understood him knew. But this evening his gratitude seemed a gift of small account. The ear was deaf and what thanks of his could reach it? The body was dust, and in what ecstasy of his could it share? The spirit had fled, in agony and loneliness, never to know that it bequeathed him salvation. . . . As he wondered, the silence of the night was broken. The whistle of Mr. Pembroke's train came faintly and a lurid spot passed over the land—passed and the silence returned. One thing remained that a man of his sort might do. He bent down reverently and saluted (his) child; to whom he had given the name of their mother.

Forster does not always make his attitude so clearly felt.

But here, remembering what Mr. Pembroke has represented all through the book—convention, rigidity of mind, meanness—it is unmistakeable; "a lurid spot passed over the land—passed and silence returned." The life of earth, the intuitive free honest life remains.

This contrast between the life of freedom and the conventions is brought out sharply in *Where Angels Fear to Tread*, a novel which also gives a great deal of Forster's very delicate comedy. Here the free life is represented by the Italian Gino, the man who marries Lilia a rather stupid Englishwoman, for her money, and thus rouses the attention and displeasure of Lilia's English relatives, who come out to Italy after her death there in order to rescue her child from his Italian father.

Gino symbolizes for Forster the spirit of Italy—as Philip Herriton says when Lilia goes on her first journey there:

> I do believe that Italy really purifies and ennobles all who visit her. She is the school as well as the playground of the world. . . . There was something half attractive, half repellent, in the thought of this vulgar woman journeying to places he loved and revered. Why should not she be transfigured? The same had happened to the Goths.

So the theme is set and from this the story develops. Italy makes the barbarian Lilia marry the son of an Italian dentist—unromantic enough. But from this all the rest happens, including the spiritual regeneration of Philip.

Gino, then, the man who marries Lilia for her money, the half-educated, uncultured, limited man, yet represents the spirit of Italy. He is cunning, avaricious, cruel, but his feelings and motives are, like Stephen's, "pure" (again in the chemical sense). This is what differentiates him sharply from the Herritons and their friend Miss Abbott, who act as they do not from desire or conviction but because they have accepted the conventional attitude, taken over the stock way of thinking. For example, when Caroline Abbott interviews Gino to put before him their proposal to take his child and Lilia's back to England, Gino says that he won't consent to part from his son:

> "For they would separate us," he added.
> "How?"
> "They would separate our thoughts."
> She was silent. This cruel, vicious father knew of strange refinements. The horrible truth, that wicked people are capable of love, stood naked before her, and her moral being was abashed. It was her duty to rescue the baby, to save it from contagion, and she still meant to do her duty. But the comfortable sense of virtue left her. She was in the presence of something greater than right or wrong.

Compare with this the similar sentiment expressed in *The Longest Journey* when Rickie at last realizes that a sound relationship with Stephen is possible:

> He believed that the earth had confirmed him. He stood behind things at last, and knew that conventions are not majestic, and that they will not claim us in the end.

Again, in *Where Angels Fear to Tread*, Forster openly contrasts the two methods of existence, the conventional and the free, by placing them side by side with an ironic comment. Monteriano, where Gino lives, is thus described as Philip approaches it:

> As they climbed higher, the country opened out, and

there appeared high on a hill to the right, Monteriano. The hazy green of the olives rose up to its walls, and it seemed to float in isolation between trees and sky, like some fantastic ship city of a dream. Its colour was brown and it revealed not a single house—nothing but the narrow circle of the walls, and behind them seventeen towers—all that was left of the fifty-two that had filled the city in her prime. Some were only stumps, some were inclining stiffly to their fall, some were still erect, piercing like masts into the blue. It was impossible to praise it as beautiful, but it was also impossible to damn it as quaint.

The irrepressible Gino, in an act of gratuitous kindness, had sent a picture postcard to Irma, Lilia's child by a former marriage, whom the Herritons are bringing up:

> Irma collected picture postcards, and Mrs. Herriton or Harriet always glanced first at all that came, lest the child should get hold of something vulgar. On this occasion the subject seemed perfectly inoffensive—a lot of ruined factory chimneys—and Harriet was about to hand it to her niece when her eye was caught by the words on the margin ("View of the superb city of Monteriano—from your litel brother").

"A lot of ruined factory chimneys." . . . "It seemed to float in isolation between trees and sky, like some fantastic ship city of a dream"—the two views are deliberately opposed. Monteriano in the Herriton atmosphere is reduced to sordidness.

This is Forster's favourite method of indicating his own view. There is in his work an extremely subtle and constant juxtaposition of opposing values. Sometimes the mood of detachment, humour, or farce is predominant, as when the news of Lilia's engagement comes to the Herritons who are upset and cross:

> Lunch was nasty; and during pudding news arrived that the cook, by sheer dexterity, had broken a very vital knob off the kitchen range. "It is too bad," said Mrs. Herriton. Irma said it was three bad and was told not to be rude. "I am going to the kitchen" (said Mrs. Herriton), "to speak about the range."
>
> She spoke just too much, and the cook said that if she could not give satisfaction she had better leave. A small thing at hand is better than a great thing remote, and Lilia, misconducting herself upon a mountain in central Italy, was immediately hidden.

Again, when the letter containing the news of Lilia's marriage arrives, Mrs. Herriton and Harriet are sowing peas in the garden. They are thrown into agitation and go into the house to make plans:

> Just as she was going upstairs (that evening) she remembered that she never covered up those peas. It upset her more than anything, and again and again she struck the banisters with vexation. Late as it was, she got a lantern from the toolshed and went down the garden to rake the earth over them. The sparrows had taken every one. But countless fragments of the letter remained, disfiguring the tidy ground.

Thus by two ironic comments, the value of the Lilia situation to Mrs. Herriton is made plain—on a par with trouble with the cook, and the interruption of good gardening. But in Italy the situation is not so neatly disposed of. It grows significant, until it involves an entire change of attitude on the part of two people, Caroline Abbott and Philip; and the death of the child about whom the trouble arose. The world of these people will never be the same again. Philip speaks:

> As yet he could scarcely understand the thing. It was too great. Round the Italian baby who had died in the mud there centred deep passions and high hopes. People had been wicked or wrong in the matter; no one save himself had been trivial. Now the baby had gone, but there remained this vast apparatus of pride and pity and love. For the dead, who seem to take away so much really take with them nothing that is ours. The passion they have aroused lives after them, easy to transmute or transfer, but well-nigh impossible to destroy. And Philip knew that he was still voyaging on the same magnificent, perilous sea, with the sun or the clouds above him, and the tides below.

This insistence on the importance of non-triviality, of passionately desiring or passionately acting, is a corollary to the main emphasis on the "natural" life, and comes out again and again in the novels. It appears for example in Philip's final realization of what Mrs. Herriton and her way of life—the conventional, stereotyped world—really amounts to:

> Her life, he saw, was without meaning. To what purpose was her diplomacy, her insincerity, her continued repression of vigour? Did they make anyone better or happier? Did they even bring happiness to herself? Harriet with her gloomy peevish creed, Lilia with her clutches after pleasure, were after all more divine than this well-ordered, active, useless machine.

The same comment of course and the same attitude behind it is seen in Rickie's reaction to Mrs. Failing in *The Longest Journey*, and in the significant remark on his own behaviour:

> It seems to me that here and there in life we meet with a person or incident that is symbolical. It's nothing in itself, yet for the moment it stands for some eternal principle. We accept it, at whatever cost, and we have accepted life. But if we are frightened and reject it, the moment, so to speak, passes; the symbol is never offered again.

This attitude, again, is at the basis of *A Room with a View*, where Lucy's muddle proceeds from her refusal to accept the moment of harmony with George as being valid; and appears most explicitly of all in Caroline's words to Philip towards the end of *Where Angels Fear to Tread*:

> "Every little trifle" (she says), "for some reason does appear incalculably important today, and when you say of a thing that "nothing hangs on it" it sounds like blasphemy. There's never any knowing (how am I to put it?) which of our actions, which of our idlenesses won't have things hanging on it for ever."

And of course in this book the whole crisis turns on an apparently trivial happening.

This is obviously an attitude extremely important to Forster—the need for vital response, wholeness, whole participation, significance—and ought to be remembered when one comes to *A Passage to India*.

It is natural perhaps that a belief in violent action or violent feeling should go along with this—at any rate in these three early novels, and in *Howard's End*, the presence of sudden irruption of passionate feeling, violent accident, or sudden death, is very marked. The Italian who is stabbed in front of Lucy and George's eyes in a moment (in *A Room with a View*), the death of the baby (in *Where*

Angels Fear to Tread), Leonard's sudden death (in *Howard's End*), Gerald's sudden death on the playing field (in *The Longest Journey*)—all these are neither accidental nor unimportant. It underlies Forster's attitude fundamentally, and perhaps Rickie's words when the tram which he and his friends are *not* in, overturns on its way from Cambridge station and a passenger is killed, serve to bring this out:

> "In his short life Rickie had known two sudden deaths, and that is enough to disarrange any placid outlook on the world. He knew once for all that we are all of us bubbles on an extremely rough sea. Into this sea humanity has built as it were, some little breakwaters—scientific knowledge, civilized restraint—so that the bubbles do not break so frequently or so soon. But the sea has not altered, and it was only a chance that he, Ansell, Tilliard, and Mrs. Aberdeen had not all been killed in the tram.
>
> They waited for the other tram by the Roman Catholic church. . . . It watches over the apostate city, taller by many a yard than anything within, and asserting, however wildly, that here is eternity, stability, and bubbles unbreakable on a windless sea."

The approach indicated in the last sentence, however, is not Forster's. He points, as well as anyone, to that collapse in the structure of the modern world with which Dr. Richards deals in the chapter on beliefs in *Principles of Literary Criticism*, and more especially in *Science and Poetry*. But one of the most interesting things about Forster's work is that in the later novels there is an attempt to substitute something else for the religious sanction—"asserting . . . that here is eternity, stability, and bubbles unbreakable on a windless sea." This is done partly, of course, in the early novels, by the attitude to the harmony or "rightness" attained by the free life, the "integral" life of feeling. But Forster is able to discard or modify an attitude which he discovers, through time or change in experience, to be too uncompromising. There is thus a continual feeling of growth and progression in the novels, even though the main theme may be fairly constant.

2

To take the modification of this attitude first. The insistence on the value of free response is justified radiantly at the conclusion of *A Room with a View*, justified soberly in *The Longest Journey*, and apparently left wavering in *Where Angels Fear to Tread*. This novel deserves some further discussion as it is very important from this point of view—in some ways it foreshadows the view taken in *A Passage to India*, and may help to elucidate some of the vexed questions which that book raises.

Caroline Abbott and Philip Herriton are the people in *Where Angels Fear to Tread* with a spark of imaginative intuition, who go through an experience in Italy—an apparently trivial experience—which alters the whole world for them. They try to rescue Lilia's child and are not successful; Harriet steals the child; the carriage in which they take it away upsets in the mud, and it is killed. Gino the father tries in insane grief and fury to kill Philip; Caroline intervenes and the two men are reconciled. The English people return to England.

At one point in the tale, Caroline and Philip meet in the church of the little town when, after Philip has felt the liberating influence of feeling at the Italian theatre, he is beginning to be aware, as he afterwards puts it, of "the vast apparatus of pride and pity and love" involved. They talk together; Philip speaks:

> "Going to the theatre yesterday, talking to you now—I don't suppose I shall ever meet anything greater. I seem fated to pass through the world without colliding with it or moving it—and I'm sure I can't tell you whether the fate's good or evil. . . . Life to me is just a spectacle."
>
> She said solemnly, "I wish something would happen to you, my dear friend, I wish something would happen to you."
>
> "But why?" he asked smiling. "Prove to me why I don't do as I am."
>
> She also smiled, very gravely. She could not prove it. No argument existed. Their discourse, splendid as it had been, resulted in nothing, and their respective opinions and policies were exactly the same when they left the church as when they had entered it.

It is impossible here not to be reminded of that conversation between Miss Quested and Fielding in *A Passage to India*, where the same detachment, the same negation of romantic feeling, is implied, but one step further in the negative direction. Fielding and Miss Quested in the later book may be taken in a sense to symbolize sanity, good-will, common sense (at this point in the tale at least)—and they have been drawn together after the disastrous incident in the trial of the Indian when Miss Quested's honesty destroys the charge against him:

> "I want to go living a bit."
>
> "So do I."
>
> A friendliness, as of dwarfs shaking hands, was in the air.

Both man and woman were at the height of their powers, sensible, honest, even subtle. They spoke the same language and held the same opinions, and the variety of age and sex did not divide them. Yet they were dissatisfied. When they agreed, "I want to go on living a bit," or "I don't believe in God," the words were followed by a curious backwash as though the universe had displaced itself to fill up a tiny void, or as though they had seen their own gestures from an immense height—dwarfs talking, shaking hands and assuring each other that they stood on the same footing of insight.

Again this sort of distrust comes out, to revert to *Where Angels Fear to Tread*, in Philip's feelings after the crisis:

> Life was greater than he had supposed, but it was even less complete. He had seen the need for strenuous work and righteousness. And now he saw what a very little way these things would go.

This, however, is not the last statement in that most interesting book. The final sentences are a supreme achievement, on Forster's part, of the balancing or inclusion of the two opposing attitudes. As they are in the train going back to England, Caroline tells Philip of her love for Gino just as Philip is beginning to hope that his love for her may be returned. Forster goes beyond the merely personal question of Philip's disappointment:

> Out of this wreck there was revealed to him something that was indestructible. . . . This episode which she thought so sordid, and which was so tragic for him, remained supremely beautiful. To such a height was he lifted, that without regret he could now have told her that he was her worshipper too. But what was the use of telling her? For all the wonderful things had happened.

"Thank you," was all that he permitted himself. "Thank you for everything."

She looked at him with great friendliness, for he had made her life endurable. At that moment the train entered the San Gothard tunnel. They hurried back to the carriage to close the windows lest the smuts should get into Harriet's eyes.

When one remembers that all through the book Harriet has symbolized conventionality, dullness, triviality, and that these are the last sentences of the book, it is clear that they illustrate Forster's power of ironic detachment, of including the point of view most in opposition to the feeling he is communicating. He does not erect his world of feeling on a false basis; he makes allowance for the materialism, the convention, the pettiness which he hates and opposes; he reckons with it instead of suppressing it.

One might however conclude from the end of this book that a kind of disillusion was setting in, the disillusion which seems to have been, as far as critics were concerned, the most important feature of *A Passage to India*.

But before discussing this most important novel, something must be said about *Howard's End*, a book which seems to stand by itself half-way between the early novels and the last one. In this novel we first openly come on the emphasis on the value of personal relationships—the second substitute, as it were, for the religious sanction—a value implied though not stressed in the other novels. It is latent in them and comes out occasionally specifically, as in Rickie's final acceptance of Stephen, in Philip's attitude to Gino at the end, in the relationship between Lucy and George. For Forster, as for Lawrence, personal relationships are only possible when accompanied by a realization of the complete integrity, so to speak, of the other person involved.

> Even when we love people we desire to keep some corner secret from them, however small; it is a human right; it is personality. (*The Longest Journey*.)

Sometimes it comes out by an expression in general terms:

> In public life who shall express the unseen adequately? It is private life that holds out the mirror to infinity; personal intercourse, and that alone, that ever hints at a personality beyond our daily vision." (*Howard's End*.)

In *Howard's End* this is what underlies the whole scheme; Margaret and her sister realize the sacredness of personality; the Wilcoxes do not. The Wilcoxes are Forster's materialists, the whole family, with the notable exception of Mrs. Wilcox, being practical, prosperous, unimaginative. Henry Wilcox is almost the worst. Yet he marries Margaret, whose values are essentially those of the non-conventional world, and Forster leaves us in no doubt finally as to the sympathy between them. The materialist in Henry, it is true, has first to be broken by violent circumstances; but what is remarkable in this book is that, unlike all the earlier ones, there is a deliberate association between the people who stand for completely different attitudes—between the Wilcoxes, and Margaret and her sister. And the regeneration of the Wilcoxes is asserted almost at the expense of the justification of "pure" feeling as exemplified by Helen and Leonard. There is no longer a complete opposition between them, as there is between what George stands for against Cecil,

Gino against Mrs. Herriton, Stephen against Mr. Pembroke. In this respect this novel indicates a much more inclusive, much more mature point of view than the others. It is indeed Forster's most valuable book, if we except *A Passage to India*, partly because of its tone of reconciliation, of the harmony of opposites.

Further, the characters who symbolize free as against conventional feeling, have altered and become much more individual. In the early books, Stephen, Gino, George, are all comparable and have the same essential features in common. There is no one quite of that kind in *Howard's End*. But the person who represents the "right" attitude, is the first Mrs. Wilcox, who loves Howard's End like a person and bequeaths it to Margaret as her spiritual heir. Mrs. Wilcox appears in the flesh very little, once to bring harmony out of a quarrel, once to awaken Margaret to awareness, but all through the book and after her death her influence is apparent, in something of the same way in which Mrs. Ramsay's is in *To the Lighthouse*. She has an extraordinary influence, yet she is after all, as Forster is at pains to make clear, a very ordinary person.

In this respect Mrs. Wilcox is a central figure in Forster's work. She recalls Rickie's mother in *The Longest Journey*, and anticipates that most important character, or perhaps "presence" would be a better word than "character," Mrs. Moore, in *A Passage to India*; *Howard's End*, in this respect, marks a moment of pause for Forster before *A Passage to India*. In it he has deliberately stressed the value of personal relationships—implicitly gathering up in that a great deal of the ideas on non-conventionality expressed in the earlier books, and asserting this as being the only kind of stable basis for existence. In *A Passage to India* personal relationships appear to be doubted.

This last book which—as far as the novels are concerned—appeared after a silence of fourteen years, and which ostensibly deals with the difficulties of communication and understanding between East and West, this last book has been hailed by critics as representing the post-War attitude of despair and disillusion and disintegration, as well as anything could. Certainly, as one would expect, the tone is different from the free comic overflow of the earlier novels. But it is a case of development rather than of change; and though naturally, because the writer is older, the tone is more meditative, less impassioned, and therefore with more emphasis on ironic detachment, the *general* conclusions it reaches may be found to be the same as in the earlier novels, with certain modifications.

The earlier novels substitute belief in the life of impulse for the religious belief. *Howard's End* substitutes belief in personal relationships. *A Passage to India* subtly seems to deny complete belief both in personal relationships and in the free way of living. What it offers positively is Mrs. Moore and what she stands for.

Mrs. Moore is the perfectly ordinary and at times rather tiresome old lady who accompanies Adela Quested to India, who after the Marabar Caves episode leaves her, and on the voyage home to England in the hot season, dies on board ship. Like Mrs. Wilcox, she has very little, practically, to do with the events that take place. But her influence subtly remains with everyone she has met, and with a great many people she hasn't met; and Forster, sometimes with his tongue in his cheek, sometimes perfectly seriously, almost exalts her to the role of presiding deity.

It is to Mrs. Moore that the experience in the Marabar caves happens, the experience of disillusion, of utter negation of value:

> She had come to that state where the horror of the universe and its smallness are both visible at the same time—the twilight of the double vision in which so many elderly people are involved. If this world is not to our taste, well at all events there is Heaven, Hell, Annihilation—one or other of those large things, that huge scenic background of stars, fires, blue or black air. All heroic endeavour, and all that is known as art, assumes that there is such a background, just as all practical endeavour, when the world is to our taste, assumes that the world is all. But in the twilight of the double vision, a spiritual muddledom is set up for which no high-sounding words can be found; we can neither act nor refrain from action, we can neither ignore nor respect infinity. Mrs. Moore had always inclined to resignation. As soon as she landed in India it seemed to her good. . . . To be one with the Universe! So dignified and simple. But there was always some little duty to be performed first, some new card to be turned up from the diminishing pack and placed, and while she was pottering about, the Marabar struck its gong.
>
> . . . . .
>
> The echo in a Marabar cave is entirely devoid of distinction. Whatever is said, the same monotonous noise replies, and quivers up and down the walls until it is absorbed into the roof. "Boum" is the sound as far as the human alphabet can express it, or "bou-oum," or "ou-boum"—utterly dull. Hope, politeness, the blowing of a

nose, the squeak of a boot, all produce "boum." . . . Mrs. Moore did not wish to repeat that experience. The more she thought over it, the more disagreeable and frightening it became. She minded it much more now than at the time. The crush and the smells she could forget, but the echo began in some indescribable way to undermine her hold on life. Coming at a moment when she chanced to be fatigued, it had managed to murmur, "Pathos, piety, courage—they exist and are identical, and so is filth. Everything exists, nothing has value."

I cannot accept the view enunciated by many critics that in that passage Forster's complete philosophy is expressed. Taken by itself, it does seem to indicate a weary resignation, an acceptance of the negation of value, a despair, which brings its author into line with the Eliot of *The Waste Land*. Admitting the significance of the passage, I yet think it fairer to accept it in its context, and with reference to other remarks in the book itself, as well as outside it. It is very important, for example, to remember that on Mrs. Moore's journey through India en route for England, there is a counteracting effect:

There was for instance a place called Asirgarh which she passed at sunset and identified on a map—an enormous fortress among wooded hills. . . . What could she connect it with except its name? Nothing; she knew no one who lived there. But it had looked at her twice and seemed to say, "I do not vanish." "I have not seen the right places," she thought (as she neared Bombay). . . . As she drove through the huge city she longed to stop . . . (but) the feet of the horses moved her on, and presently the boat sailed and thousands of coco-nut palms appeared all round the anchorage and climbed the hills to wave her farewell. "So you thought an echo was India; you took the Marabar caves for final?" they laughed. "What have we in common with them, or they with Asirgarh?"

Combined with Mrs. Moore's later influence, this seems to me evidence dangerous to neglect. At the trial it is a sudden remembrance of her that makes Adela withdraw her accusation against Aziz, to the scandal of the European colony and her own disgrace. At the trial also, the Indians waiting outside have seized on Mrs. Moore's name and have turned it into a kind of ridiculous invocation:

> The tumult increased, the invocation of Mrs. Moore continued, and people who did not know what the syllables meant repeated them like a charm. They became Indianized into Esmiss Esmoor . . . a Hindu goddess.
>
> "Esmiss Esmoor
> Esmiss Esmoor
> Esmiss Esmoor
> Esmiss Esmoor."
>
> Suddenly it stopped. It was as if the prayer had been heard, and the relics exhibited.

This idea is further amplified after the news reaches India of Mrs. Moore's death—with a good deal of seriousness underlying the lightness of the tone:

> (Her) death took subtler and more lasting shapes in Chandrapore. . . . At one period two distinct tombs containing Esmiss Esmoor's remains were reported; one by the tannery, the other up near the goods station. Mr. McBryde visited them both and saw signs of the beginning of a cult—earthenware saucers and so on. Being an experienced official he did nothing to irritate it, and after a week or so, the rash died down. "There's propaganda behind all this," he said, forgetting that a hundred years ago, when Europeans still made their home in the countryside

> and appealed to its imagination, they occasionally became local demons after death—not a whole god perhaps, but part of one, adding an epithet or gesture to what already existed, just as the gods contribute to the great gods, and they to the philosophic Brahm.

Finally, it is the memory of Mrs. Moore which causes the reconciliation between Aziz on the one hand, and Fielding and Mrs. Moore's children on the other, with which the book ends. Significantly, too, Mrs. Moore's image appears momentarily to old Professor Godbole, the Indian philosopher, when he is striving, through Krishna worship, to attain a mystic harmony with the God.[1]

In the face of all this, I find it impossible to agree that Forster's final, and possibly his most important, book expresses only that sense of disillusion which had begun to be marked in *Where Angels Fear to Tread*, and which receives its most open and precise expression in the Marabar caves passage here. It seems to me much more probable that this book sums up a great deal of what I have tried to show as Forster's characteristic point of view in all his books. The belief in a pagan freedom has been modified, the belief in personal relationships has been as it were sublimated—Mrs. Moore represents a more subtle and complicated form of communication, of sympathy, of "vision." When Adela talks to Fielding of the cave episode and Aziz' innocence, she acknowledges that she herself does not really yet know what happened :

> "Mrs. Moore—she did know."
> "How could she have known what we don't?"

[1] This has an obvious affinity with that incident in *To the Lighthouse*, where Mrs. Ramsay, after her death, appears to Lily Briscoe.

"Telepathy, possibly."

The pert, meagre word fell to the ground. Telepathy? What an explanation. . . . Perhaps life is a mystery, not a muddle.

All through his work, Forster, as I have tried to show, contrasts and brings together two opposing points of view which one may conveniently call the "romantic" and the "ironic." In doing so he makes very clear his own preference for the "romantic," the "impulsive," the "integral" mode of feeling. In *A Passage to India*, a much more complicated book, admittedly his preference is not so marked, but to a careful reader that attitude is at least as strong as the supposed mood of complete disillusion, of negation of value. The book, in fact, gives an extreme instance of his general method, and, it is interesting to note, the opposing attitudes are here united in the person of Mrs. Moore—she represents the mystery as well as the muddle, helps to point the ironic detachment, the intellectual aloofness, as well as the sympathy, the mysterious significance, with which Forster is concerned.

This is not a mean achievement, to obtain completeness out of such dissonant elements. The combination of intellectual detachment, of humorous observation, is not often found very closely allied with what Wordsworth calls the "visionary mood." That Forster manages to place them both in juxtaposition without causing either to be exaggerated or untruthful constitutes his claim to the possession of a distinctive attitude, an attitude which is worthy of serious consideration.

THE NOVELS OF D. H. LAWRENCE

Lawrence is a curiously uneven writer. There is no novelist of today who shows more obvious signs of power and imagination—the dark, poetic power of a Webster—nor one who at times can write so badly and think so carelessly. His books come as though straight off the pen, and one of their outstanding characteristics is their naturalness and spontaneity. When the emotion behind the writing is urgent and compelling, the style becomes molten and glows with heat; at other times it is colloquial and loose. Lawrence writes out of himself; he does not rely on intellectual comprehension, but on an intuitive emotional apprehension of reality, communicated forcibly and convincingly as he feels it.

One of his greatest gifts is his power of description, especially of natural description, in active quick prose, unforced and vivid. And again, perhaps one should say of him, as one says of Keats, that no understanding of Lawrence is possible without an intimate knowledge of his letters. I do not intend, however, to deal with either of these aspects now, but to concentrate on his central ideas as expressed in the novels.

His books are disturbing—violent, bitter, contemptuous

—but in them one can discover an attitude, the expression of which is extremely personal but which has a certain definite and general value. He is preoccupied with the problem of sex, possessed by it as Webster was by the idea of death, and almost all his books are attempts to grapple with the problem and to find a solution. And this is connected with his other, later preoccupation, the problem of man's adjustment to the universe—both important and huge themes; and whether Lawrence is right or wrong, at least he is positive in the statement of his beliefs. He achieves most when he relies not on explicit statement or theorizing but when he lets his characters find their own expression and response to a situation. But in every one of his books the same essential problem (whether explicit or latent) is set forth, and a similar means of solution either found or indicated.

There are three chief "beliefs" or convictions which continually recur: (1) The value of direct physical sensuous feeling as against an intellectual understanding, "heart" as against "head" knowledge. (2) The value of *violent* feeling, as for instance, hate, as essentially bound up with love and at times affording an equal satisfaction. (3) The necessity for the individual to be separate, single, self-complete even at the moment of most intimate union with another individual. There is obviously a fallacy in the second conviction; here he makes the mistake of equating *violent* with *deep*—the two are by no means necessarily synonymous. There is undoubtedly a sadistic element in Lawrence—it comes out perhaps most typically in that poem, often quoted, not by any means his best but characteristic of this side of him:

Under the long dark boughs, like jewels red
  In the hair of an Eastern girl
Hang strips of crimson cherries, as if had bled
  Blood-drops beneath each curl.

Under the glistening cherries, with folded wings
  Three dead birds lie;
Pale-breasted throstles and a blackbird, robberlings
  Stained with red dye.

Against the haystack a girl stands laughing at me,
  Cherries hung round her ears.
Offers me her scarlet fruit: I will see
  If she has any tears.

These three "beliefs," however, appear continually in Lawrence's work; it is interesting to trace their development from the first real novel, *The White Peacock*, to the later books where at times the artistic presentation suffers because of the violent and angry intrusion of theory.

The White Peacock in a sense stands by itself. It is completely different in tone from any of the other novels, being conceived in a mood of reverie, the lyrical passive mood which feels the flow of life and its regrets as much in the changing features of a loved landscape as in the lives of men. It is a kind of prose poem—the poetic apprehension of life that is a tangle and unhappy, but that has exquisite moments. There are in it flaws and lapses typical of an early work, but as a whole it stands by itself as the expression in one mood of a musing on life—Lettie, Leslie, Emily, Cyril are shadows on the golden landscape, and represent that sinking into the rich life of earth which is characteristic of Lawrence. But if this is true of the book as a whole, it must also be said that in it the kind of reality with which Lawrence afterwards deals enters from time to time—Sam and the keeper's household are as pressingly alive as anything could be. And the tragic incursion of Tom into this passive world of wistful longings and troubled acceptance of life is very real and very disturbing. It is noticeable indeed that though the book is sharply differentiated from the others that follow, it yet contains the faint beginnings of some of their prepossessions. The characters are in a sense the first sketches for those in *Sons and Lovers*—the situation between Emily and Cyril is the foreshadowing of that between Paul and Miriam, although in *The White Peacock* it is not so complex nor so distressing. Alice is exactly the counterpart of Beatrice, who flashes into life for a few moments in the scene in Paul's kitchen, and is moreover brought in to point the same contrast, between her careless acceptance of life and Emily-Miriam's shrinking from and brooding on it. The encounter between Leslie and Lettie before their marriage is another thing which is out of character but typical of Lawrence. What is really unessential to the movement of *The White Peacock* as a whole, becomes the dominating theme of the later books—the struggle between man and woman, between man and himself, to effect a balance that will make both sides richer, more complete and self-fulfilled.

Sons and Lovers is on the whole his best achievement, although again it is not quite in line with the later development. But it is an artistic triumph. In it what afterwards becomes a specialized theme is treated broadly and with a deep and searching appeal. Paul's specific experience may not be that of everyone, but Paul's relationships with Miriam and Clara on the one side and with his mother on the other, are, generally, true. The first awaking of passion, the strain and bewildered clash of temperament between Paul and Miriam, the surfeit and frustration of passion with Clara, the agony of his mother's death, and Paul's feeling of despair and of a meaningless world—all these carry their own sharp reality and value with them. It is almost the only novel of Lawrence's which is complete in itself, each part necessary to the rest—it is noticeable for example how the early scenes with the struggle between Mrs. Morel and her husband are inevitable both psychologically and artistically for the truth of the account of Paul's later development. The book is obviously based (how obviously can be corroborated by reading "E. T.'s" biography) on actual experience, and it impresses one painfully but magnificently with its truth and its power.

It is different with all the later books except *The Rainbow*. The early part of *The Rainbow* rests on Lawrence's own experience, and there is a tenderness in its sensuous feeling which is unusual in his writings. There is also a sharp and new observation of the possible relationship between man and woman which makes its pressure felt convincingly. The first part of *The Rainbow* is written out of satisfied senses; in it Lawrence contributes something new and valuable. The second part seems to me less important, less vital; the characters of Gudrun and Ursula re-appear, grown-up, in *Women in Love* and one can trace if one wishes to follow that kind of experiment, their ways of behaviour back to their roots in the first novel. But it is the first part which contains the essential Lawrence; he wrote of it in a letter: "It is really something new in the art of the novel," and again, "Primarily I am a passionately religious man, and my novels must be written from the depth of my religious experience." The suppression of the book when it first appeared must have affected him with anger and distrust. Nothing Lawrence ever wrote afterwards has this tone of sensuous ease, of *gratification*, in Blake's sense; and every later book is either bitter or defiant.

Both *Sons and Lovers* and *The Rainbow*, then, have been written out of a sharp, vital experience. In the other novels the direct experience is fitful and they are more or less formulations of a theory about human relationships. *Sons and Lovers* is concerned with the problem of sex—but not entirely. Paul's relations with both Miriam and Clara are stages in his development, and, on the whole, are perhaps not so important as the binding and dominant tie between him and his mother (a very interesting autobiographical detail; Lawrence obviously suffered from a "mother-complex"). What is important in the book and what it seems to stress, is Paul's attitude to life after all these experiences. There is no attempt to utter any explanation or criticism of conduct; but the last sentences of the book are an imaginative and luminous record of the capacity of the individual for suffering and struggle:

> "Where was he?—one tiny upright speck of flesh, less than an ear of wheat lost in the field. He could not bear it. On every side the immense dark silence seemed pressing him, so tiny a spark, into extinction, and yet, almost nothing, he could not be extinct. Night in which every-

> thing was lost, went reaching out, beyond stars and sun. Stars and sun, a few bright grains, went spinning round for terror, and holding each other in embrace, there in a darkness that outpassed them all, and left them tiny and daunted. So much, and himself, infinitesimal, at the core a nothingness, and yet not nothing. . . .
>
> But no, he would not give in. Turning sharply, he walked towards the city's gold phosphorescence. His fists were shut, his mouth set fast. He would not take that direction, to the darkness, to follow her. He walked towards the faintly humming, glowing town, quickly."

This *general* truth is not what the other novels are concerned with. In all of them Lawrence's sensitive response to Nature, his lively and evocative expression of the scenes, people, places he himself has directly observed, can be found, but more and more fragmentarily. He is not content to give shape and form to his attitude towards experience and his evaluation of it merely by means of and through the actions, thoughts and expressions of his characters: he is more and more concerned with an explicit expounding of his "beliefs" or theories on the central problem of sex—a problem which seems at times to block out any other consideration. This is what partly accounts for the fact that the later books are all more or less jerky, ill-balanced, incomplete—the ideas come so fast and are expressed so quickly that there is not time to weld them together into a coherent shape. Perhaps in any case they would not form so; perhaps what is valuable in them is the leaping, white-hot intensity of feeling which lies behind them.

The three most important books from the point of view of a theory of relationships, are *Women in Love*,

Aaron's Rod, and the long short-story *The Captain's Doll*. If *Sons and Lovers* is Lawrence's best book, *Women in Love* is the most typical, both of his faults and his virtues—the astonishing looseness and carelessness of expression and construction, and the equally astonishing power of lighting up detail and incident with the clearness of something actually seen. All his theories can be found here, sometimes expressed implicitly in character revelation, sometimes openly and explicitly by comment or expression in his own voice. The insistence on the *violent* emotions and their expression in physical outbursts is remarkable—*e.g.* Hermione's attempt to crush Birkin [compare with this, the queer climax of *The Fox*, where the soldier kills Banford]; Birkin's fight with Gerald; the astonishing quarrel on the roadside between Birkin and Ursula. It is of course preoccupied with sex, and strives towards a resolution of the problem in harmony. This harmony just fails of attainment—and only just. Perhaps in no other book is the conflict seen more clearly or a clearer revelation given that "love," for Lawrence, is not to be equated with mere instinctive animalism. Middleton Murry seems to me to have misunderstood the intention of this novel completely.[1] On one side Gudrun and Gerald [who may be said to represent "the heart," *i.e.* direct reliance on purely physical feeling], on the other Ursula and Birkin, try to find a satisfying way of life. Gudrun and Gerald attempt to find self-fulfilment through sexual desire, through the satisfaction of physical passion, but the connection between love and hate is so near that at last they realize one or the other of them must in the

[1] *Son of Woman*, Middleton Murry (Cape, 1931), pp. 112–122.

process be destroyed. Ursula and Birkin, as an immediate contrast, find harmony because their union is not based merely on physical intimacy but on the assumption (at any rate on Birkin's part) of the value of each personality's being distinct and separate, even at the height of passion. ["He said the individual was *more* than love or than any relationship. For him, the bright single soul accepted love as one of its conditions, a condition of its own equilibrium."] It is curious to find this attitude in the author of the *Lost Girl*, a book which seems to justify the heart (*i.e.* direct feeling) versus head (*i.e.* the power to "will" feeling, to feel at second hand), in its perfect reliance on, and contentment with, the things of the senses. But Birkin's utterance, subtly enough, is not an entire negation of feeling. The Hermione-Birkin situation collapses because of Hermione's insistence on the "power to will": the Gerald-Gudrun situation collapses because of their entire reliance on direct and intense feeling: the Birkin-Ursula situation is valid because, loving each other, they realize that each personality is entirely separate.

This singleness and separateness of the individual is emphasized again in *Aaron's Rod*, a book full of the disintegration and despair of the after-war world. How vividly the experiences—Aaron's abandonment of his wife, his journeys in Italy, the discussions with the Englishmen he meets, the disturbances of the Italian peasants, rise up before one, as a background for the expression of his development, through sexual experience, to a different and more satisfying outlook. "He realized that he had never intended to yield himself fully to her or to anything . . . that his very being pivoted on the fact of his isolate self-responsibility, aloneness. His intrinsic and central aloneness was the very centre of his being. Break it, and he broke his being."

One might compare with this, a late novel *Kangaroo*, where there is, characteristically, a most realistic and moving account of the horrors of suspicion and discomfort which a conscientious objector had to suffer in wartime England, and where the chief theme of the book, though not so directly expressed, is Somers' effort to retain his "self-possession" in the new country of Australia where men are brotherly and free and seek to establish contact. The individualism which is shown, is, if pushed to extremes, definitely anti-social; but in the world of the artist it is the individual who counts. The contrast between the world of reality and the world of art, in this respect, is at times too difficult a matter for Lawrence: there is an intrusion of actual life into theory and vice versa, in the novels, which makes them at times artistically poor. Nevertheless the underlying idea is both true and valuable.

Of all the novels mentioned so far, none quite succeeds in composing the different elements and forming a definite and satisfying attitude to life. But in the *Captain's Doll* this is effected. It happens that here there is not only a revelation of Lawrence's meaning by means of the relations of the characters, but also in an explicit series of statements, made by the Captain, who speaks in, and not out of, his character. That is, the book combines successfully an artistic and a "philosophic" presentation of the persistent problem—the adjustment of man to woman, and so of each to life. The explicit statements form four stages of realization, and each stage can be found in the other novels. The first comes when Hepburn gives himself up to his love for Hannele: "Words mean so little. They mean nothing. And all that one thinks and plans doesn't amount to anything. Let me feel that we are together and I don't care about all the rest." [This is obviously paralleled in the relationships between Gerald and Gudrun, Paul and Clara, and the characters in *The Lost Girl*.]

The second stage occurs after the shock of his wife's death. "It affected him with instantaneous disgust when anybody wanted to share emotions with him. He did not want to share emotions of any sort. He wanted to be by himself, essentially, even if he was moving about among other people." [Parallel statements can be found throughout such novels, for instance, as *Aaron's Rod, Women in Love, Kangaroo*.]

The third stage comes as the development of a new attitude, directly springing from the second: "We must all be able to be alone, otherwise we are just victims. But when we *are* able to be alone, then we realize that the only thing to do is to start a new relationship with another—or even the same—human being. That people should all be stuck up apart, like so many telegraph poles, is nonsense." This is the reiteration of the central belief at the basis of the character of Paul, Birkin, Somers, and is evidently one of the most stressed and constant. With it as a corollary there goes the almost hysterical denial of love, the utter revulsion of feeling away from its confinement and enchainment to a freer realization of the difficult but satisfying balance of two personalities. And so comes the fourth stage: "If a woman loves you she'll make a doll out of you. She'll never be satisfied till she's made your doll. And when she's got your doll, that's all she wants. And that's what love means. And so, I won't be loved, and I won't love. I won't have anybody loving me. It is an insult . . . I'll be honoured and I'll be obeyed: or nothing." (Compare *Women in Love*, *Aaron's Rod.*) Perhaps it is worth saying again that to Lawrence "love" in this sense means a falsification of the deeper impulses, a falsification which springs from the mind and its notions.

Detached from its context this may seem ridiculous or absurd; in its context it is illuminating and critical. It is difficult to detach the "ideas" in a book from the book itself, and often dangerous. Lawrence has the poet's power of expressing his feelings about life in symbols—the embodied and palpable forms of his characters. He is most successful artistically when his characters are allowed to speak for themselves and to us, directly, out of their own situation. But with all the flaws and confusions into which Lawrence's thought, or rather, intuition leads him, one is able to gather from the novels—not a systematization of conduct—but a consistent way of dealing with experience, a consistent attitude to life. *The Captain's Doll* expresses fully what almost all the other novels express in part; direct contact by means of emotion has been tried and found wanting: the individual finds himself to be more than any one of his experiences, even than the experience of love; but individual relationships with others are necessary to the fulfilment of personality. Hence the conception of a relationship which will consist of the reciprocal balance and poise of two "self-possessed" entities, and will so afford both freedom and completion of the personality.

This is a valuable conception, but it is not enough for Lawrence. *The Captain's Doll* is not altogether typical of his attitude. The major problem of man's adjustment to the universe he finds himself in, still has to be solved. This for Lawrence was connected with the problem of finding a leader, and in *Psychoanalysis and the Unconscious* he has much to say on this point which lights up his doctrine in some of the later novels, notably in *The Plumed Serpent*. Lawrence was interested in the problem of personal adjustment because for him it implied something more than mere personality. He writes for instance in a letter:

> You mustn't look in my novel for the old stable *ego* of the character. There is another *ego*, according to whose action the individual is unrecognizable, and passes through, as it were, allotropic states which it needs a deeper sense than any we've been used to exercise, to discover are states of the same single radically unchanged element.

And this state of what he elsewhere calls "lapsed consciousness" when the self is swallowed up in the general dark flow and rhythm of life, is emphasized again and again, sometimes in that peculiar phraseology which makes him for some readers irritating—for instance the passage about Kate's feeling in *The Plumed Serpent*:

> She would begin to approximate to the old mode of consciousness, the old, dark will, the unconcern for death, the subtle dark consciousness, non-cerebral, but vertebrate. When the mind and the power of man was in his blood

and his backbone, and there was the strange dark inter-communication between man and man and man and beast, from the powerful spine.

Lawrence hates and despises the modern mechanical world and its values and tries to set up a new world and a new value. But in order to do this he proceeds backwards. Just as in his theory of human relationships he relies basically on this dark sympathetic "polarity" which has nothing to do with the mind, so in establishing a new Atlantis he draws on the dark primitive state of tribes away from the corrupting influence of civilization. In *The Lost Girl* there is a passage which anticipates—although the tone is not yet one of complete acquiescence—the theme which is developed in *St. Mawr*, *Mornings in Mexico*, and *The Plumed Serpent*[1]:

> "It seems there are places which resist us, which have the power to overthrow our psychic being. It seems as if every country had its potent negative centres, localities which savagely and triumphantly refuse our living culture. And Alvina had struck one of these, here on the edge of the Abruzzi . . . and yet, what could be more lovely than the sunny days: pure, hot, blue days among the mountain foothills. . . . Nothing could have been more marvellous than the winter twilight. Sometimes Alvina and Pancrazio were late returning with the ass. And then gingerly the ass would step down the steep banks, already beginning to freeze when the sun went down. And again and again he would balk the stream, while a violet-blue dusk descended on the white, wide stream-bed, and the scrub and lower hills became dark, and in heaven, oh, almost unbearably

[1] *Psychoanalysis and the Unconscious* gives a rationalized statement of his views and is very important in this connection. Compare Lawrence's three centres of life with the Yogi.

lovely, the snow of the near mountains was burning rose, against the dark-blue heavens. How unspeakably lovely it was no one could ever tell, the grand pagan twilight of the valleys, savage, cold, with a sense of ancient gods who knew the right for human sacrifice. It stole away the soul of Alvina. She felt transfigured in it, clairvoyant in another mystery of life. A savage hardness came in her heart. The gods who had demanded human sacrifice were right, immutably right. The fierce savage gods who dipped their lips in blood, these were the true gods."

In *The Plumed Serpent* the old gods of Christianity are useless; it is time to look for new gods, for the godhead which is in every man when he is in full accord with the deep natural rhythm of the earth:

The sun has climbed the hill, the day is on the downward slope.
Between the morning and the afternoon, stand I here with my soul, and lift it up.
My soul is heavy with sunshine, and steeped with strength.
The sunbeams have filled me like a honeycomb,
It is the moment of fullness,
And the top of the morning.

Here the two ideas of "leadership" or "godship" and of the primitive blood-bond with natural forces, unite in a poem which has something of the fervour and imagery of the prophets of the Old Testament. In this novel—which is perhaps the most explicit statement of his belief that we have—the theme is treated with a great deal of imaginative vigour. One of the most striking passages occurs near the beginning where Kate voyages down the lake and the quiet unfolding of life, the instinctive peace of Nature is contrasted with the disintegration of the so-called "civilized" world. There are times when Lawrence seems to be a wilder and more savage Wordsworth, with a similar power of evoking the actual experience. As the book progresses, however, it seems to me to decline in force. The emphasis on blood-contact, the primitive emotional reaction to the tom-tom beating, Ramon's hymns—all these lack a final impressiveness. Lawrence tries very hard to make us believe that his solution is the final one, but one cannot help suspecting that he is at the same time trying to persuade himself. Ramon, who represents his views best, is really conscious of defeat. As for the lesser figures, Kate and Cipriano, they are extremely unsatisfactory: Kate comes over to the new religion very half-heartedly and wavers in her allegiance to it: and her marriage to Cipriano seems to be due to nothing more than physical impulse, though Lawrence tries to invest it with mysterious significance.

The novel is a failure—but a gigantic one, which shows Lawrence's power as well as his limitations. In it, as in all his work, there is a remarkable indictment of some of the false values of modern life; a deep sense of the mystery and religious character of the most important experiences of life, including sex; and a conviction that life cannot be lived fully unless one is in harmony with the rhythmical flow of natural forces, the movement of the sun and of the seasons. All of these are valuable notions, which contain more than a grain of truth. By his power as a novelist and even more by his power as a poet (and here I am not thinking of the poems)—in spite of incoherence, over-emphasis and violence—Lawrence forces us to listen to him and to think.

THE TRAGIC IN HARDY AND CONRAD

BOTH Conrad and Hardy seem in a sense a little old-fashioned if one puts them beside contemporary names—Joyce, Hemingway, dos Passos, Faulkner, Powys; but they are important as having, in contrast with most of the writers of this century, a profound tragic sense. Both deflect tragedy a little, into a new course, by a subtle alteration of its elements; Hardy, by an emphasis on both bitterness and pity; Conrad, by a combination of romanticism and irony. I shall attempt only a few remarks on Hardy before going on to a more general survey of Conrad.

Hardy may be regarded as a sort of pioneer in the modern novel; one should remember that in his day he was regarded as "advanced" and revolutionary—*Tess of the d'Urbervilles* on its appearance was regarded with suspicion, and *Jude the Obscure* is obviously a propagandist novel, propagandist in respect of ideas. A whole ferment of new social ideas and criticism of the old order lies behind many of his books. Equally obvious is his feeling for the country, especially one particular locality, and intimately bound up with that, his feeling for the kind of individual who is as it were the particular "tree walking" of that locality—such characters as Gabriel Oak, Clym Yeobright, Diggory Venn, Marty South, all of whom, like Wordsworth's Michael, seem to spring out of and endure with the landscape which is their background. One might indeed take as a motto for Hardy's novels those lines of Wordsworth's:

> Suffering is permanent, obscure and dark,
> And shares the nature of infinity.

The comparison with Wordsworth is by no means fortuitous. Hardy has been said to be Wordsworth a hundred years older and wiser, and there seems to be a regular progression from Wordsworth's attitude to nature, with its emphasis on *joy*, through Arnold, who echoes while repudiating, as in the lines:

> He sees life unroll
> A placid and continuous whole;
> That general life which does not cease,
> Whose secret is *not joy, but peace*.

and so to Hardy who would have substituted instead of peace, something like endurance or fortitude. Endurance or fortitude in the face of an ironic and even spiteful universe, for of course Hardy's universe is controlled by powers who, as he indicates at the end of *Tess*, mock at mankind.

I say this because critics have made a great deal of the pessimism which seems to spoil the tragic tone of the novels; but ought one not rather to say it is this very pessimism that gives *specific* tone, that tone of astringent bitterness which marks Hardy's shift of the tragic emphasis? Tragedy turns in his hands not "to favour and to prettiness" but to labour and to bitterness. It is true, however, that in his novels the odds are weighted against the characters too mechanically by means of accident. The preponderance of fatal accident in Hardy's world is of course notorious, and in *Jude the Obscure* especially it seems to be oppressively and inartistically emphasized. In spite of many extremely fine things in that book—and its realism and starkness divide it off sharply from any lesser work; it is very much a book of ideas and of modern ideas—in spite of this, the mechanical handling of the characters in order to bring out Hardy's accusation against the universe, lessens its value. I mean for instance the unintelligence shown by such an intelligent character as Sue in moments of crisis; her actions seem out of keeping with the character as previously delineated.

The words "view of the universe," not a phrase which troubles most of the moderns very much (except Lawrence), are essential for Hardy. He is a serious tragic artist concerned with those issues and presenting to us characters also so concerned. When one points out that in his novels the plot seems conditioned by accident, such notorious accidents as the mislaid letter in *Tess*, Clym's absence from home when his mother makes her last journey over the moor, the small fatal chances in *The Mayor of Casterbridge*, one has also to say that, in accordance with Aristotle's profoundly true statement, the characters are essentially the cause of their own destiny. That a character is what it is, of course, can be pushed back out of its control to rest on heredity and environment, and Hardy emphasizes this semi-fatalistic attitude markedly. But this "accidental" inheritance is not only legitimate but important, on a tragic view, and it is this which in its turn produces Hardy's profound pity for the *nature* of mankind.

What is perhaps more important is Hardy's emphasis on natural as against social law, and here too he tends to over-stress both in *Tess* and *Jude*, bitterly inveighing against social conditions which drive Tess, his "pure woman" as he himself calls her, to destruction or which result in the Elizabethan holocaust of *Jude the Obscure*. This of course, while it gives a curiously dated air to his work,[1] also makes him valuable as a social novelist of a time which has not yet, in spite of many reforms, quite passed by. But allowing for this, his general and permanent value lies rather in his presentation of a tragic character against his natural background in a way in which both largeness and accurate truth are combined. Nothing could be more exquisite than the change from the idyllic atmosphere of those dairy scenes in *Tess* which breathe the richness and content of earth, to the later starve-crow farm where she gains her hard living. When one thinks of someone with whom to compare Hardy, one has to turn to the greatest names, to the epic con-

[1] It is very interesting to compare Hardy in this respect with "Mark Rutherford," whose view is in some respects more modern and more intellectual. I am thinking here of his (M. Rutherford's) treatment of Madge in *Clara Hopgood*, who realizes that the momentary act of passion with Frank is something not integral to her character and which therefore cannot be permitted to act as a conventional inhibition on her life; she therefore refuses to marry him, having surveyed the situation with her full *intelligence*, whereas Tess (her weakness and strength both lying in this) acts only through her natural instincts. All Hardy's characters who break the social law suffer, sometimes inartistically and unjustifiably.

ception of Tolstoi, the dramatic conception of Shakespeare. Michael Henchard in *The Mayor of Casterbridge* is like those stormy heroes of Shakespeare, Macbeth or Othello, the man of passion whose many good qualities are undermined by one fatal flaw and circumstance. Henchard is a superb example of the true tragic character, from his first appearance selling his wife in a drunken impatient fit at the fair, through his triumphant rise to power (the comparison of the structure of the book is with the curves of a play and shares something of that concentration), to that last glimpse of him as he makes his way out of the town, degraded, solitary, wretched. His self-written epitaph in its savage bareness and pride echoes the nature which has been its own downfall and has roused both pity and fear:

MICHAEL HENCHARD'S WILL

That Elizabeth-Jane Farfrae be not told of my death, or made to grieve on account of me.
& that I be not bury'd in consecrated ground.
& that no sexton be asked to toll the bell.
& that nobody is wished to see my dead body.
& that no murners walk behind me at my funeral.
& that no flours be planted on my grave.
& that no man remember me.
To this I put my name.

MICHAEL HENCHARD.

It is this power of representing both passion and pity (*& that no man remember me*) which ultimately constitutes Hardy's claim to greatness. In spite of the sometimes too explicit bitterness, the almost intellectually dishonest use of contrived circumstance (Hardy's substitute for the *diabolus ex machina*), in spite of this, pity and fear, the Aristotelian desiderata, are fused in his novels to a new amalgam. Perhaps pity predominates, as for instance Henchard's pathetic last attempt to visit his daughter with a present of a goldfinch which he leaves "under a bush outside to lessen the awkwardness of his arrival." When he is repulsed by Elizabeth-Jane and turns in bitterness away from the house, the cage is left behind and discovered some days later—"a new bird-cage, shrouded in newspaper, and at the bottom of the cage a little ball of feathers—the dead body of a goldfinch." Hardy's power of conveying tenderness for the particular person or thing through the statement of a stony and barren philosophy may be seen more concentratedly in that exquisite little poem *Proud Songsters* (itself reminiscent of Wordsworth's

> Rolled round in earth's diurnal course
> With rocks and stones, and trees).

This is the poem:

> The thrushes sing as the sun is going
> And the finches whistle in ones and pairs,
> And as it grows dark, loud nightingales
>   In bushes
> Pipe, as they can, when April wears
> As if all Time were theirs.
>
> These are brand-new birds of one year's growing
> Which a year ago or less than twain,
> No finches were, nor nightingales,
>   Nor thrushes,
> But only particles of grain
> And earth and air and rain.

Behind its apparent simplicity is a complex attitude—stoic acceptance of the inanimate origin and return of animate life; a feeling of pity and tenderness for the creatures momentarily so vital, *as if all Time were theirs*, when the irony is both in the fact that they have so little of it, and that they are unconscious of the dusty end which awaits them; and, surprisingly, a hint, since earth and air and rain are integral elements for *life*, of the miraculous re-birth from nothingness. One thinks of that compassionate comparison in Bede, of the duration of man's life as like a sparrow's flight in winter through a warm lighted hall, from darkness to darkness. It is the impression of Hardy's *humanitarianism* which finally remains with one—pity for man and his sufferings, pity intensified by his consciousness of the unfairness both of man's surroundings and of his own make-up.

Conrad, with whom Hardy has much in common,[1] is impelled by a different purpose—to show the tangle, the inexplicable element in life. For this purpose he invents in some of his most important novels the figure of Marlowe, the shadowy ideal spectator who tells the story as he sees it. By means of him the story can be told with the effect of conversational ease and with a wealth of detail otherwise impossible; we see the incidents as it were coming to life, beating themselves out in his mind

[1] Here I must acknowledge my indebtedness to Dr. Richards, who first pointed out to me that pity and fear in Conrad are very subtly altered, so that the emphasis is laid finally on something which I should call "admiration."

I must also thank Dr. Richards for first directing my attention to the importance of the scene with Stein in *Lord Jim*.

as it discovers and illuminates truth. Marlowe can obviously be compared with the ideal spectator of Henry James who uses his "beautiful intelligence" to sort out the complicated pieces of the puzzle; just as in James, the complexity and difficulty of the process is emphasized, and the simplicity of the final result. This method of gradual accretion in the mind of one person is useful not only to show the intricacy of problems of behaviour but also to give a framework, to detach the problem from immediacy. We see Flora in *Chance* or Lord Jim in the novel of that name as it were at one remove because through the eyes of Marlowe, and an effect of distance or perspective is given. (The most modern development of this method is perhaps Gide's *Les Faux Monnayeurs*, a novel, as Edwin Muir calls it, about a novelist writing a novel.) This technique is especially useful in a book like *Chance* whose main theme is the exposure of all possible variations in a given problem of adjustment, in order to show how mysterious and unaccountable human behaviour is—a theme and method which has affinities with Browning's in *The Ring and the Book*. In this way the tragic figure of Flora de Barral is slowly and indirectly presented to us so intimately as almost to be felt like oneself; and every detail of her unfortunate position, friendless in a world where friendship is one of the supreme gifts and the most secure (a favourite emphasis of Conrad's to which I shall return later) is told so as to bring out the perplexity and tangle of human affairs. In *Lord Jim* this narration from inside is not so successful; Marlowe is in place throughout the first part which is on the whole meditative, but in the second part which is more important and more passionate, the method occasionally breaks down. In *Heart of Darkness*, however, that short story which must be placed among the most typical and best of all Conrad's writing, it is entirely successful. The story is of a young man who sails up lonely reach after reach in the darkest forest of Africa past various outposts of progress and civilization until he reaches the final one of all set in the heart of the dark land; there he sees Kurtz, the manager whom he has come to meet and who is regarded as a pioneer of light only to find him degraded and obsessed with the most horrible rites of native witchcraft. Whether a personal experience lies behind this or not, the power with which a sense of the evil and sinister is conveyed is extremely impressive. Method and subject in this tale are equivalent; the quiet reflective narration only emphasizes the more the sudden shock with which the dark enchanted figure of Kurtz is finally revealed—enchanted in the sense in which Coleridge uses it, the drawing, magical power of evil. In this tale there is an important symbolic emphasis on the mystery of the human voice, seen for example in one of the early descriptions of Kurtz:

> Of all his gifts the one that stood out pre-eminently, that carried with it a sense of real presence, was his ability to talk, his words—the gift of expression, the bewildering, the illuminating, the most exalted and the most contemptible, the pulsating stream of light, or the deceitful flow from the heart of an impenetrable darkness.

This is emphasized at point after point in the tale so that Kurtz, by a cumulative effect becomes as it were a voice crying in the wilderness, a voice finally of the most sinister revelation. The most dramatic and concentrated part of the story occurs at the end when, after Kurtz's death, Marlowe visits Kurtz's fiancée in England:

> I thought his memory was like the other memories of the dead that accumulate in every man's life—a vague impress on the brain of shadows that had fallen on it in their swift and final passage; but before the high and ponderous door, between the tall houses of a street as still and decorous as a well-kept alley in a cemetery, I had a vision of him on the stretcher, opening his mouth voraciously as if to devour all the earth with all its mankind. He lived then before me; he lived as much as he had ever lived—a shadow insatiable of splendid appearances, of frightful realities; a shadow darker than the shadow of the night, and draped nobly in the folds of a gorgeous eloquence. . . . And the memory of what I had heard him say afar there, with the horned shapes stirring at my back, in the glow of fires, within the patient woods, those broken phrases came back to me, were heard again in their ominous and terrifying simplicity. . . . I seemed to hear the whispered cry, "The horror! The horror!" . . .

Marlowe enters the house to find Kurtz's fiancée (who has some of the nobility of the later heroines) overcome with grief and anxious to recapture any memory he possesses of the final end of the man she loved:

> "No," she cried. "It is impossible that all this should be lost—that such a life should be sacrificed to leave nothing—but sorrow. You know what vast plans he had. I knew of them too—I could not perhaps understand—but others knew of them. Something must remain. His words, at least, have not died."
>
> "His words will remain," I said. . . . She said suddenly very low, "He died as he lived."

"His end," said I, with dull anger stirring in me, "was in every way worthy of his life."

"And I was not with him," she murmured. My anger subsided before a feeling of infinite pity.

"Everything that could be done——" I mumbled.

"Ah, but I believed in him more than anyone on earth—more than his own mother, more than himself. He needed me! Me! I would have treasured every sigh, every word, every sign, every glance."

I felt like a chill grip on my chest. "Don't," I said, in a muffled voice.

"Forgive me. I—I—have mourned so long in silence—in silence. . . . You were with him—to the last? I think of his loneliness. Nobody near to understand him as I would have understood. Perhaps no one to hear . . ."

"To the very end," I said shakily. "I heard his very last words. . . ." I stopped in a fright.

"Repeat them," she said in a heart-broken tone. "I want—I want—something—something—to—to live with."

I was on the point of crying at her, "Don't you hear them?" The dusk was repeating them in a persistent whisper all around us—in a whisper that seemed to swell menacingly like the first whisper of a rising wind. "The horror! The horror!"

The *irony* of this passage about Kurtz is superbly done, and has in its context an enormous effect. It is different from Hardy's use, at once more open and more subtle, and done for a different purpose, to bring out the mysterious darkness, the baffling *duality* of man's nature. This is very important when one comes to consider later Conrad's view of the world and the stress he lays on faith and honesty. [A somewhat comparable use of irony is seen in *Victory*—there is a symbolic emphasis here on Lena's voice, the symbol, unlike Kurtz, of innocence;

YES

and Conrad's curious combination of romanticism and irony (to be seen later much more subtly in Lord Jim) is brought out by this emphasis—her voice is for Heyst both salvation and destruction; but for it the tragedy would not have happened; but for it, likewise, Heyst would not have been regenerated.]

Conrad however is master not only of this subtle method of procedure in the tales where Marlowe figures but of quiet and straightforward narrative, and also of a sort of atmospheric and romantic effect. Indeed he has come to be almost identified with this last style, and to be regarded with disfavour on that account. Later, I hope to show that Conrad himself in *Lord Jim* (in many ways his most important book) gives a very subtle exposure of the problem of "romanticism" and suggests its cure. At the moment I wish to consider the group of short stories and novels in the romantic "*genre.*" As a first example, one might take the short story called *The Inn of the Two Witches*—it is in its way a perfect accomplishment, even though its way is that of melodrama—the English sailor on the unknown Spanish coast, the suspicious gaiety of the lowland innkeeper, the disappearance of the Englishman's servant, his apprehensive arrival at nightfall at the dark Inn of the Witches set by itself on an impassable track in the heart of the hills—the atmosphere of suspicion, of strangeness, of fear is wonderfully caught throughout; as an excursion into the fantastic, even if the excursion runs on fairly well-known lines, it is perfectly done. This power of creating atmosphere can be seen, more admirably, in *The Nigger of the Narcissus.* Here the effect produced is that on the minds of a ship's crew by one of their number, a nigger, who refuses to work because Death may claim him at any moment; when he dies and his body is cast overboard, the spirit of unrest and mutiny which has hung over the ship seems to lift away like a cloud, as though the emanation of the spirit of revolt and antagonism had been contained in the lonely desperate figure of James Wait, with his queer pride in his companion Death. The comparison which suggests itself here is a poetic one, with the *Ancient Mariner*, a comparison which has also been claimed, rightly I think, for *The Shadow Line*, where a ship seems to refuse to pass the latitude where the body of her late captain lies buried, and where the atmosphere of the supernatural and uncanny is given by a few suggestive touches.

Conrad is generally concerned with the unanalysable, the intangible, which exists as a vast background to the rational and explicit. When not under strict control, this interest leads him into a kind of pseudo-romanticism, often co-existing with the authentic one, as I think happens in *Victory* and again in *The Rover*; and "purple patches" of a rhetorical kind can occur even in a novel mainly straightforward. Conrad was not by any means a "pure" artist, as his style shows; that turbid, over-decorated, over-cadenced style which can however at its best produce the flashlight revelation of poetry—as for instance in *The Rescue* or *Nostromo*,—and which has an extraordinary range of evocative imagery. Perhaps it would be true to say that though Conrad's settings, particularly in the tropics, may be almost as romantic as a fairy-tale, yet in his actual studies of human beings he never strays far from reality. Even in the early *Almayer's*

Folly, where the heat seems to shimmer like a transparent veil over the characters, the blaze of colour and luxuriance serves chiefly as a background for the passionate story of Nina and Dain—a meaningful background; Nina is in keeping with her setting and one thinks of her as of a brilliant-plumaged bird of Paradise. The colour is more glaring, more violent here than in the later books, but the sombre reverse side is seen in the melancholy, warped life of Almayer and in the suggestion of native craft and guile—a note struck with more insistence and with a deeper effect of horror in *Heart of Darkness*.

Generally speaking, Conrad is most romantic in stories whose setting is in the tropics, and most realistic in those where the background is the sea, although sometimes both modes combine in one book. His descriptions of the sea are unrivalled, in its shiftings of mood and its terrors. The very feeling of a storm is given in, for instance, *The Nigger of the Narcissus*, when the ship is beating round the Cape, and nothing but dogged perseverance saves the crew, or in *Typhoon*. And we are given, too, the spirit of unswerving devotion which characterizes the real sailor. Like Hardy's knowledge of the Wessex peasant, Conrad's knowledge of the sailor is bound up with his environment; there is a bond between the sea and the man who labours on it, they complement each other, just as the landscape in Hardy is the natural complement to the earth-worker. The picture is given faithfully with the accuracy which Conrad's own early experiences would furnish, and the vividness which belongs to his creative power. He is aware of the cruelty, as well as the allure, of its fascinations.

Yet his main interest is not in the background, but in the individual lives of particular men, though generally he is conditioned in his choice just as Wordsworth was, by interest not so much in the individual variations as in the broad similarities which ultimately emerge. This may be to place the emphasis wrongly, however. It would certainly be wrong not to stress the *range* of Conrad's delineation of men, their actions and feelings given to us by a dramatic situation or set of situations, or revealed in the long-drawn-out, leisurely, intricate reminiscence of Marlowe—Captain Whalley, Tom Lingard, Razumov, Heyst, Lord Jim, Kurtz—they are all different and all differentiated. As a rule the chief characters are men, but Conrad can draw exquisite portraits of women. Flora de Barral is herself the centre of the conflicting mesh of circumstance with which *Chance* is concerned, that book of patient searching out of inmost motive; in *Under Western Eyes* Natalie is almost as important as Razumov. His women are purely feminine beings, emotional but not sentimental, and especially endowed with sympathetic understanding; passionate sometimes, though rarely; austere, but with a gracious sweetness behind the austerity; of the type of Hermione rather than Cleopatra. But again what a range! From Natalie Haldane the stern young enthusiast with her passion for simple truth, to Mrs. Gould's delicate tenderness which conceals an immense capacity for suffering.

But the women, delicately etched portraits as they are, do not have the place in the tales which belongs to the men. And it is true to say that the *final* impression which emerges from the romantic, the intricate or the plain direct approach is one, perhaps as Henry James might have said, of the *surroundedly* labyrinthine maze, and emphatically of the fundamental simplicity of the response. All the tales are in essence accounts of a single soul's adventures. This is very clearly seen in the group of novels and stories characterized by quiet and straightforward narrative. Conrad, whose main characteristic is an exuberant richness, knows how to be sparing in his words and at times achieves almost an epic simplicity. The short story called *The End of his Tether* is direct and unvarnished in its poignancy, but the two chief examples of this bare style are of course *Under Western Eyes* and *The Secret Agent*. The latter book is perhaps a *tour de force* rather than anything else, but *Under Western Eyes* surely deserves to rank, in its different way, with *Chance*. The undecorated anguish of Razumov becomes almost intolerably piercing, until it is with a sense almost of physical relief that one hears of the end of his mental sufferings after confession—for the bodily suffering which directly ensues seems of small account compared with the agony of indecision with which he has been tortured.

The plot of this book reveals one of Conrad's fundamental and recurring ideas—the theme, here of conscience, elsewhere of duty. In a greater or less degree the same theme comes out continually. Here, for instance, Razumov the hard-working, industrious student has to choose between sheltering an anarchist who is his friend and who seeks his house uninvited to hide, and betraying him to the authorities. After stormy deliberation with himself, he takes the latter course, and spends the rest of his life trying to escape from the atmosphere of intrigue and suspicion with which he is surrounded as the result of the violation of his word. Again, the situation in *The Rescue* is a similar one, though the emphasis here is rather on the press of life and circumstance which enchain a man; yet here too it is a case of faith broken which brings about the catastrophe. But of course the most notable example is *Lord Jim*; this is very important and therefore calls for some further discussion. Jim is a youth whose imagination is too strong for his sense of duty, and who therefore in a crisis, by a momentary instinctive action, done almost without realization, abandons his sinking ship and saves his life. What the book relates is his inward rehabilitation, to put matters right with himself, to set constantly such an ideal of honour before himself and to follow it, that he may have the confidence of knowing that he can trust his own strength. An ordinary idea enough. The interest lies in an unusual emphasis on Conrad's part. Lord Jim is obviously a romantic; he fails to act in a situation of danger because of his miserable imagination of what *might* happen. His friend Marlowe seeks advice on his behalf from a shrewd old friend of his, a German scientist, the collector of butterflies, to whom he presents Jim's case as another "specimen" to be analysed. The answer given is a profound one, and the passage where it occurs is of central significance in the book; one which shows Conrad's awareness of his own romantic prepossessions, and one which symbolizes both the cure for romantic fancy and also the necessity for the fierce self-discipline implied:

> When I finished he uncrossed his legs, laid down his pipe, leaned forward towards me earnestly with his elbows on the arms of his chair, the tips of his fingers together.

"I understand very well. He is romantic."

He had diagnosed the case for me, and at first I was quite startled to find how simple it was; and indeed our conference resembled so much a medical consultation—Stein, of learned aspect, sitting in an arm-chair before his desk; I, anxious, in another, facing him, but a little to one side—that it seemed natural to ask:

"What's good for it?"

He lifted up a long forefinger.

"There is only one remedy! One thing alone can us from being ourselves cure!" . . . "We want in so many different ways to be," he began again. "This magnificent butterfly finds a little heap of dirt and sits still on it; but man he will never on his heap of mud keep still. He want to be so, and again he want to be so. . . ." He moved his hand up, then down. . . . "He wants to be a saint and he wants to be a devil—and every time he shuts his eyes he sees himself as a very fine fellow—so fine as he can never be. . . . In a dream . . . I tell you, my friend, it is not good for you to find you cannot make your dream come true, for the reason that you not strong enough are, or not clever enough. . . . A man that is born falls into a dream like a man who falls into the sea. If he tries to climb out into the air as inexperienced people endeavour to do, he drowns—nicht wahr? . . . No! I tell you! *The way is to the destructive element submit yourself,*[1] and with the exertions of your hands and feet in the water make the deep, deep sea keep you up. So if you ask me—how to be?"

His voice leaped up extraordinarily strong, as though away there in the dusk he had been inspired by some whisper of knowledge. "I will tell you! For that too there is only one way. . . . *In the destructive element immerse.*"[1] . . . He spoke in a subdued tone, without looking at me, one hand on each side of his face. "That was the way. To

[1] The italics are mine.

follow the dream, and again to follow the dream—and so—
ewig—usque ad finem. . . ."

And so Lord Jim follows *his* dream of honour *usque ad finem* and finds the logical end in death. Marlowe's words at the end of the book sum up the problem with delicate discrimination and with a profoundly subtle ironic undertone:

> And that's the end. He passes away under a cloud, inscrutable at heart, forgotten, unforgiven, and excessively romantic. . . . He goes away from a living woman to celebrate his pitiless wedding with a shadowy ideal of conduct. Is he satisfied—quite, now, I wonder? . . . Now he is no more, there are days when the reality of his existence comes to me with an immense, an overwhelming force; and yet upon my honour there are moments too when he passes from my eyes like a disembodied spirit astray amongst the passions of this earth, ready to surrender himself faithfully to the claim of his own world of shades.

The loneliness and the hazard of life are continually being stressed by Conrad, and the implacable responsibility of each soul to itself. Like Hardy, he has a profound feeling for the tragic; he sees life as a dark mystery, where evil and good flourish side by side, where men cannot realize the vast consequences of their own tiny actions, or have any real understanding of the minds of their fellow-men. But almost always, unlike Hardy, man is represented as "himself the author of his proper woe." It is no mean tragedy which Conrad sees played out before him—man is faulty but he has also a breath of elemental greatness in him. The essential value lies not in the tragic fault but in the temper of the hero, the aspiration and striving towards an ideal which encompasses and yet escapes him. *Endeavour* is one of the watchwords of Conrad's faith; and duty, loyalty, courage are virtues which loom largely in his world. There is something here which invites a Shakespearean comparison. Everywhere he sees goodness bound up with evil, and cessation from goodness leads to untold loss. His idea of goodness, as Shakespeare's, is something in the last resort fundamentally simple. Man must do his utmost to preserve order; without order—one is reminded of *Troilus and Cressida*—everything would fall to pieces, be wasted. Duty and faith are ways of preserving the ultimate order of things, ways of giving stability to a world attacked by the forces of disruption. Charles Gould's remark in *Nostromo*, the most Shakespearean in tone of all the novels, on the unrest of the South American republic with which he has to deal, may be taken to signify Conrad's view of life:

> What is wanted here is law, good faith, order, security.

Both Hardy and Conrad might be adduced as a corrective to that disintegration which is to be found, as Virginia Woolf herself stated most clearly, in contemporary writers—a corrective which includes, in its complexity, both bitterness and irony as elements of strength.

MOORE AND JOYCE
A CONTRAST

No better contrast could be found than these two writers, who are alike perhaps only in two things, that they are Irish and that they are prose-writers. In Moore the Irish background is only secondary; he very obviously derives from France, as his wit, his sharp intelligence, his lack of sentiment show. He is an admirable foil to his fellow-nationalist, beside whose Pilgrim's Progress or Odyssey of the soul, *Ulysses*, Moore's *Ave atque Vale* seems almost like a child's playing with toys.

Yet Moore cannot be dismissed lightly. He has something of Horatian elegance, of the intelligence of the eighteenth century, the witty impudence and urbanity of Pope, something too of the observant eye of Chaucer, but of the malicious Chaucer in whom coarseness and urbanity are combined. He is essentially critical and destructive, and in him the pure play of intelligence seems to become something rather decadent, a self-disintegrating force. This is I think because in him the artistic and the personal self exist as it were on different levels, and because he is fundamentally un-serious.

His first important work, however, *Esther Waters*, is an exception, and an admirable exception. It is a sympathetic study of "low life" done with an accurate and understanding eye, and, particularly if read in comparison with Hardy's *Tess*, brings out Moore's especial virtues. He expresses in this book something of the patient passive suffering of the non-intellectual, the "animal" nature, that is heart-rending in its dumb acceptance of misery. But at the same time he shows also in Esther's character and in the attitude of the others, a power of adaptation, of common sense (one might almost say of horse sense), of prose reaction to the situation, which is utterly different from the poetic and tragic feeling of Hardy. Moore is fundamentally incapable of tragedy; but his treatment of the theme here has much of the sober virtue of inexhaustible common life.

His formal artistry, shown later most exquisitely and subtly both in *Héloïse and Abélard* and *The Brook Kerith*, can be very easily perceived here by placing in juxtaposition the opening and close of the tale. These are the opening sentences which first bring Esther to our notice:

> She stood on the platform watching the receding train. The white steam curled above the few bushes that hid the curve of the line, evaporating in the pale evening. A moment more and the last carriage would pass out of sight, the white gates at the crossing swinging slowly forward to let through the impatient passengers.
>
> An oblong box painted reddish-brown and tied with a rough rope lay on the seat beside her. The movement of her back and shoulders showed that the bundle she carried was a heavy one, and the sharp bulging of the grey linen cloth that the weight was dead. She wore a faded yellow dress and a black jacket too warm for the day. . . . She was laughing now, the porter having asked her if she were

> afraid to leave her bundle with her box. Both, he said, would go up together in the donkey-cart. The donkey-cart came down every evening to fetch parcels.

And these are the closing paragraphs of the book:

> The train passed across the vista, and the women wondered how long it would take Jack to walk from the station. . . . The wind was rough; it caught the evergreens underneath and blew them out like umbrellas; the grass had not yet begun to grow, and the grey sea harmonized with the grey-green land. The women waited on the windy lawn, their skirts blown against their legs, keeping their hats on with difficulty. It was too cold for standing still. They turned and walked a few steps towards the house, and then looked round.
>
> A tall soldier came through the gate. He wore a long red cloak, and a small cap jauntily set on the side of his close-clipped head. Esther uttered a little exclamation, and ran to meet him. He took his mother in his arms, kissed her, and they walked towards Mrs. Barfield together. All was forgotten in the happiness of the moment—the long fight for his life, and the possibility that any moment might declare him to be mere food for powder and shot. She was only conscious that she had accomplished her woman's work—she had brought him up to man's estate; and that was her sufficient reward. What a fine fellow he was! She did not know he was so handsome, and blushing with pleasure and pride she glanced shyly at him out of the corners of her eyes as she introduced him to her mistress.
>
> "This is my son, ma'am."
>
> Mrs. Barfield held out her hand to the young soldier.
>
> "I have heard a great deal about you from your mother."
>
> "And I of you, ma'am. You've been very kind to my mother. I don't know how to thank you."
>
> And in silence they walked towards the house.

Both are similar in tone; but between them all the

happenings of one life have been given, and a feeling of the essential similarity of the life-process, its continuity, in a new life.

Ave atque Vale however is perhaps more typical of the essential Moore. Here his art is at its freshest, with its tone of elegant witty conversational ease, not yet hardened into the conscious perfection of *Héloïse*, but alive and sprightly. He anticipates Virginia Woolf in his analysis of mental processes, the spring and irrelevance of thoughts; and in his awareness of the way in which the mind while focussing centrally on one thing, is yet conscious of a vast and sliding stream of impressions and sensations on the periphery—as for instance in this passage where dialogue, dramatic monologue and running commentary are given with a background of the enchanting glimmer and scent of a May evening in September:

> "She is quite right," I said to myself, as I took a seat under the apple-tree by the table laid for dinner under the great bough, "she is quite right. It is the only way out of the difficulty. If I wouldn't grieve my brother, I must leave Ireland. And it would be well to spread the news, for as soon as everybody knows that I'm going, I shall be free to stay as long as I please. AE will miss me and John Eglinton; Yeats will bear up manfully, Longworth will miss me. I shall miss them all. . . . But are they my kin? And if not, who are my kin? Steer, Tonks, Sickert, Dujardin—why enumerate? Ah, here is he who cast his spell over me from across the seas, and keeps me here for some great purpose, else why am I here?"
>
> "The warm hour prompted you, AE, to look through the hawthorns."
>
> "It was the whiteness of the cloth that caught my eye."
>
> "And you were surprised to see the table laid under the

apple-tree in this late season? But the only change is an hour less of light than a month ago; the evenings are as dry as they were in July; no dew falls; so I consulted Teresa, who never opposes my wishes—her only virtue. Here she comes across the sward with lamps; and we shall dine in the midst of mystery. My fear is that the mystery may be deepened suddenly by the going out of the lamps. Teresa is not very capable, but I keep her for her amiability and her conversation behind my chair when I dine alone. . . . Teresa, are you sure you've wound the lamps; you've seen the oil flowing over the rim?" She assured me that she had. "You cannot have seen anything of the kind, Teresa. The lamps have clearly not been wound." The wicket gate slammed. "Whoever this may be, AE, do you entertain him. I must give my attention to this lamp. It wouldn't be pleasant to find ourselves suddenly in the dark. It is you, John Eglinton? Well, I'm engaged with this lamp. You see, Teresa, the oil is rising; give me a match . . . Teresa and Moderator Lamps are incompatible. But next year I shall devise some system of arboreal illumination."

Moore is obviously a man of letters, with the limitations and advantages which that implies—the witty, enchanting *artificiality* of his naturalism is something which gives at times an exquisite pleasure just as an ode of Horace may. Very often of course the trifling tone conceals a good deal of malicious criticism, as for instance the amusing reported conversation with Yeats about their intended collaboration in writing a play on *Diarmuid and Grania*:

Yeats was composing, Lady Gregory said, we should have to wait for him, and we waited, till, perforce, I had to ask for something to eat, and we sat down to a meal that was at once breakfast and lunch. Yeats still tarried, and it was whispered round the table that he must have been overtaken by some sudden inspiration, and at this thought everyone was fluttered with care. Lady Gregory was about to send the servant up to know if the poet would like to have breakfast in his room, when the poet appeared, smiling and delightful, saying that just as the clocks were striking ten the metre had begun to beat, and abandoning himself to the emotion of the tune, he had allowed his pen to run till it had completed nearly eight and a half lines, and the conversation turned on the embarrassment his prose caused him, forcing him to reconstruct his scenario. He would have written his play in half the time if he had begun writing it in verse.

As soon as we rose from the table Lady Gregory told us we should be undisturbed in the drawing-room till tea-time. Thanking her, we moved into the room; the moment had come, and feeling like a swordsman that meets for the first time a formidable rival, I reminded Yeats that in his last letter he had said we must decide in what language the play should be written—not whether it should be written in English or in Irish (neither of us knew Irish), but in what style.

"Yes, we must arrive at some agreement as to the style. Of what good will your dialogue be to me if it is written, let us say, in the language of *Esther Waters*?"

"Nor would it be of any use to you if I were to write it in Irish dialect?"

Yeats was not sure on that point; a peasant Grania appealed to him, and I regretted that my words should have suggested to him so hazardous an experiment as a peasant Grania. . . . . .

"You'll allow me a free hand in the construction? But it's the writing we are not agreed about, and if the writing is altered as you propose to alter it, the construction will be altered too. . . . But there's no use getting angry. I'll try to write within the limits of the vocabulary you impose upon me, although the burden is heavier than that of a foreign language. I'd sooner write the play in French."

"Why not write it in French? Lady Gregory will translate it."

And that night I was awakened by a loud knocking at my door, causing me to start up in bed.

"What is it? Who is it? Yeats!"

"I'm sorry to disturb you, but an idea has just occurred to me."

And sitting on the edge of my bed he explained that the casual suggestion that I preferred to write the play in French rather than in his vocabulary was a better idea than he had thought at the time.

"How is that, Yeats?" I asked, rubbing my eyes.

"Well, you see, through the Irish language we can get a peasant Grania."

"But Grania is a king's daughter. I don't know what you mean, Yeats; and my French——"

"Lady Gregory will translate your text into English. Taidgh O'Donoghue will translate the English text into Irish, and Lady Gregory will translate the Irish text back into English."

This sharpness and acuteness of observation and the slyness of the humour with its touch of mocking malice (*Marry, sir, this is miching mallecho*) and its realism is perhaps the most typical aspect of Moore's writing. It combines the naughtiness of the *gamin* with intelligence and is admirable when used, legitimately, for pricking foolish bubbles or when jesting on a subject which lends itself to the mock-heroic; as, for instance, that superb comic scene when Moore and AE set out on bicycles to visit some tumuli, the supposed home of the gods in ancient peasant belief, and are involved in punctured tyres and absurd arguments about the speaking of Irish with a young man who is introduced as having blue

Celtic eyes and a Lancashire burr. Not only is there alert and pricking humour; there is also a power of expression, of rapid, colloquial and vivid prose which recalls in its ease and mastery of movement the wit and elegance, though not the seriousness, of Dryden.

Yet it would be unfair not to say that in *Ave atque Vale* other qualities are seen, which appear in the later works in more sustained fashion, among them particularly a sensuous apprehension of beauty (obvious of course in *Héloïse* and offset there by a pungent salt realism). The passage which occurs in the middle of the scene described above is as good as any to illustrate this:

> The miles flowed under our wheels. We had come so far that it seemed as if we might go on for another hundred miles without feeling tired, and the day, too, seemed as if it could not tire and darken into night. There was no sign of night in the sky, but the earth was darkening under the tall hedges; we passed a girl driving her cows homeward. She drew her shawl over her head, and I said that I remembered having seen her long ago in Mayo, and AE answered, "Before the tumuli, she was."
>
> We cycled mile after mile, descending the great road that leads into Drogheda, and as we came down the hill we saw the lamps in the main street; all the rest of the town was lost in shadow, and beyond the town a blue background, as likely as not the sea . . . if Drogheda be a seaport town.

The simplicity of the first paragraph cannot disguise its poetic feeling, any more than the irresponsibility of the last sentence, delightful as it is here, something a little flippant about its author.

And it is this impression of flippancy, of frivolousness, which is forcibly impressed on one by comparison with

Joyce. How shallow, how *impertinent* (in the Latin sense of that word) Moore's work appears beside the tortured anguish and disgust of the *Portrait of the Artist as a Young Man*. When one thinks of the *Portrait*, one remembers Keats' words in the preface to *Endymion*:

> The imagination of a boy is healthy and the mature imagination of a man is healthy; but there is a space of life between, in which the soul is in a ferment, the character undecided, the way of life uncertain. . . .

One thinks too of Yeats' verse:

> Out of Ireland have we come.
> Great hatred, little room,
> Maimed us at the start

and in particular, of another tortured and great mind, Swift. For Joyce, like Swift, is desperately aware of the horror and filth of mankind, and also of its sensual appeal. His book reveals the tortures of a nature which is both sensual and ascetic and which cannot find satisfaction in the religion which forms an essential part of its background. There is a striking comparison here between Moore's self-debate on the choice for him between Protestantism and Roman Catholicism—a self-debate which leads him into more witty, amusing, polished conversations with, for instance, Kuno Meyer:

> My argument had been repeated so often that it had become a little trite, and a suspicion intruded upon my mind as I hurried from St. Augustine, through Dante, Boccaccio, and Ariosto, that my narrative had grown weary. Or was it that Meyer, being a Professor, could not grasp at once that we must choose between literature and dogma? A perplexed look came into his face as I sketched out in

broad lines the sixteenth and seventeenth literature in France. As I was about to proceed northward through Denmark, Sweden, and Norway, Meyer asked questions which revealed the professor latent in him, and while answering him and trying to persuade him out of his professorial humours, I fell to thinking that perhaps he would enjoy himself better in a debate on the Shakespearian drama, or the debt that the dramatists of the Restoration owed to Molière. He would delight in satisfying our curiosity regarding the inevitable Mademoiselle de Scudery, whose festoons and astragals are of course plainly to be descried in the works of Pope and Prior. So do we often criticize our friend and he sitting opposite to us, little thinking how he is being torn to pieces.

How brilliant that is and how enchanting, in its combination of the lightness of Pope's touch and the good humour of the Swift of *The Battle of the Books*—or all the musings and speeches which follow, with his brother, with Ernest Longford, with Dr. Mahaffy, given with a seeming artlessness and a shrewd penetration only possible to a mind which is impudently urbane, self-poised, and detached. And then one reads the dialogue at the end of Joyce's *Portrait*:

Stephen . . . reopened the discussion at once by saying:

"I fear many things: dogs, horses, firearms, the sea, thunderstorms, machinery, the country roads at night."

"But why do you fear a bit of bread?"

"I imagine," Stephen said, "that there is a malevolent reality behind those things I say I fear."

"Do you fear then," Cranly asked, "that the God of the Roman catholics would strike you dead and damn you if you made a sacrilegious communion?"

"The God of the Roman catholics could do that now," Stephen said. "I fear more than that the chemical action which would be set up in my soul by a false homage to a symbol behind which are massed twenty centuries of authority and veneration."

"Then," said Cranly, "you do not intend to become a Protestant?"

"I said that I had lost the faith," Stephen answered, "but not that I had lost self-respect. What kind of liberation would that be to forsake an absurdity which is logical and coherent and to embrace one which is illogical and incoherent? . . . I will not serve that in which I no longer believe, whether it call itself my home, my fatherland, or my church: and I will try to express myself in some mode of life or art as freely as I can and as wholly as I can, using for my defence the only arms I allow myself to use—silence, exile, and cunning. . . . You made me confess the fears that I have. But I will tell you also what I do not fear. I do not fear to be alone or to be spurned for another or to leave whatever I have to leave. And I am not afraid to make a mistake, even a great mistake, a lifelong mistake, and perhaps as long as eternity too."

Beside this, almost clumsy in its earnestness, how shallow, how irresponsible appear all Moore's airy and perfectly executed gestures. Joyce is undoubtedly a serious moralist. I have said that one thinks of Swift in connection with him, and one is tempted also to compare him with Donne because of a certain searing quality of imagination—the Donne of the *Satires* or of the agonized doubtings in the *Divine Sonnets*; or, because of the sternness of his vision, with St. Augustine and his condemnation of the flesh. For the author of the *Portrait* and of that suffering Odyssey, *Ulysses*, is a "fallen man," one who is aware of the attraction of the body, and mortally afraid of it, who has been brought up in the ascetic, medieval view, that the material world is sinful. But for Joyce the personal problem cannot be solved by adherence to the Catholic faith, and I suppose one may say that we owe the artistic Joyce to that fact—the artistic Joyce is as it were a record of the tortured sufferings of a Swift without Swift's orthodoxy, and in both there is a similar cruelty, the savage cruelty of someone who is experiencing a mortal wound.

As a thinker, Joyce's view of evil and his position with regard to evil is a fascinating one. As an artist, what makes him important is perhaps chiefly his extraordinary power over words to render his experience. The manner which he is afterwards to develop, to the despair of critics, is seen already in the *Portrait*, in for instance the passage where Stephen walks by the water's edge (perhaps it is not too fantastic to stress the importance of the element of water for Joyce; for him explicitly in *Anna Livia Plurabelle* and implicitly throughout, without the need to embark on Freudian speculation, it is useful as a sexual symbol, and therefore as a symbol of the processes of life):

> He drew forth a phrase from his treasure and spoke it softly to himself:
>
> A day of dappled seaborne clouds.
>
> The phrase and the day and the scene harmonized in a chord. Words. Was it their colours? He allowed them to glow and fade, hue after hue; sunrise gold, the russet and green of apple orchards, azure of waves, the grey-fringed fleece of clouds. No, it was not their colours; it was the poise and balance of the period itself. Did he then love the rhythmic rise and fall of words better than their association of legend and colour? Or was it that, being as weak of sight as he was shy of mind, he drew less pleasure from the reflection of the glowing sensible world through the prism of a language manycoloured and richly storied

than from the contemplation of an inner world of individual emotions mirrored perfectly in a lucid supple periodic prose?

He passed from the trembling bridge on to firm land again. At that instant, as it seemed to him, the air was chilled, and, looking askance towards the water, he saw a flying squall darkening and crisping suddenly the tide. A faint click at his heart, a faint throb in his throat told him once more of how his flesh dreaded the cold infra-human odour of the sea; yet he did not strike across the downs on his left but held straight on along the spine of rocks that pointed against the river's mouth. . . .

There was a long rivulet in the strand, and as he waded slowly up its course, he wondered at the endless drift of seaweed. Emerald and black and russet and olive, it moved beneath the current, swaying and turning. The water of the rivulet was dark with endless drift and mirrored the high drifting clouds. The clouds were drifting above him silently and silently the seatangle was drifting below him and the grey warm air was still and a new wild life was singing in his veins. . . .

He was alone. He was unheeded, happy and near to the wild heart of life. He was alone and young and wilful and wildhearted, alone amid a waste of wild air and brackish waters and the seaharvest of shells and tangle and veiled grey sunlight and gayclad lightclad figures of children and girls and voices childish and girlish in the air.

Obviously this is written by one who is trying to make words as fluid as possible, to catch even while they disperse, shades of feeling, before the intellect has crystallized them. (First published in 1916, it must have influenced very greatly all but the very early work of Virginia Woolf.) Both in *Ulysses* and in *Anna Livia Plurabelle* the process is carried further; in both he is fascinated by the tones of the living voice and its infinite shifts and variations, and therefore in the latter he returns to what he knows best, the personal intonations of a particular Irish dialect, with the river Liffey as a sort of central spirit or emanation. (One might point out that in this interest he approaches the position of Moore and Yeats as set forth in *Ave*:

> "It is through the dialect," he (Yeats) said, "that one escapes from abstract words, back to the sensation inspired directly by the thing itself.")

The *sensation inspired directly by the thing itself* is obviously what Joyce, in common with most poets, wishes to achieve. In the close of *Anna Livia Plurabelle*, for all the first apparent difficulty, I think he is successful, and in this new and individual way:

> Can't hear with the waters of. The chittering waters of. Flittering bats, fieldmice bawk talk. Ho! Are you not gone ahome? What Tom Malone? Can't hear with bawk of bats, all the liffeying waters of. Ho, talk save us! My foos won't moos. I feel as old as yonder elm. A tale told of Shaun or Shem? All Livia's daughtersons. Dark hawks hear us. Night! Night! My ho head halls. I feel as heavy as yonder stone. Tell me of John or Shaun? Who were Shem or Shaun the living sons or daughters of? Night now! Tell me, tell me, tell me, elm! Night night! Telmetale of stem or stone. Beside the rivering waters of, hitherandthithering waters of. Night!

In *Anna Livia Plurabelle*, then, the theme of life and the life-process is expressed by means of the broken, bawdy, symbolical phrases which run rhythmically into and from each other like the flowing of the river or the current of life itself. But in most of *Work in Progress* the process is carried further. Logical transitions in structure are left out, words are added to or subtracted from words or parts of words in such a way as to make meaning difficult for anyone but the author, and the danger of purely *private* meanings is becoming obvious.

Just as in his early work he shows an almost medieval attitude towards the natural world, so in his later phase another medieval characteristic—it is very important to remember that Joyce was trained as a Jesuit and therefore in a rigidly traditional and exacting discipline—makes its appearance; it might be called an interest in grammar or rhetoric. The interest of the later Joyce is almost purely an interest in language; and from his work many developments have followed. There is a parallel movement in philosophy; the analytic school of Wittgenstein rests, one might say, on a grammatical basis. In literature Joyce has been the parent of such different children as Gertrude Stein (her automatic writing lacks the severe control of Joyce, however), Hemingway, and possibly Auden if one considers the new experiments with language and grammar which he makes in his poetry. Joyce's method is obviously to make play with free association, but whereas Virginia Woolf does this with ideas, he does it with words; and one is forced to say sometimes that his work has the interest of a clinical document rather than of art. He seems to me to be a very lonely genius, towering above most of his contemporaries in a sort of blind isolation, blind because perhaps misguided; and the importance of his great work may lie in the future rather in the hands of the psychologists as a case-book, than with writers and literary critics.

A NOTE ON KATHERINE MANSFIELD

KATHERINE MANSFIELD, in spite of the maturity and perfection of some of the tales, must be regarded as a writer of promise rather than of fulfilment. Her *Journal* reveals the fact that some time before her death she had decided for artistic reasons temporarily to give up writing, in order to write differently in the future. She was her own hardest critic and she felt a lack in her work which at that time she was unable to supply. Had she lived it seems inevitable that she would have produced something richer and more significant than even the best of her tales.

Yet as it stands, her work is unmistakeably of a high order. Like Tchekov, she was a *story-teller* of the first rank. The two have much in common but the similarity is not one of discipleship; Katherine Mansfield's individuality is impressed on everything she wrote. Yet the approach to their material is similar. Both try to arrest within the limits of the short-story, an emotion, an evanescent moment that lights up the play of character, an atmosphere, rather than to narrate an event or record a crisis. From both one obtains a sense of adjustment, of harmony.

This harmony results partly from the fact that Katherine

Mansfield does not shrink from the ugly aspects of life but accepts them as part of it. The story in *Bliss*, *Je ne parle pas français*, shows a deliberate attempt to grapple with not only the ugly but the abnormal, and though it is not a complete success, it shows a power of dealing with other people's emotions from the inside and of making an unfamiliar character live. The same sympathetic participation is seen in the stories, *Pictures*, *Life of Ma Parker*, and *The Cook's Story*, where characters from an unlovely side of life are made to reveal the poignancy and pathos inherent in them. Her way is to take a single isolated incident, a small occurrence, and to light it up with all the implications contained in it so that the full significance is interpreted. Her work is delicate, but because the sympathetic observation is unerring and profound it carries its own strength with it.

One of the most marked characteristics of her work is her acute sensibility to impressions. Like Proust, she remembers and records detail with a sensitiveness so fine and subtle that it is almost painful. All is not only observed but felt. Numerous passages in the *Journal* indicate how every impression was received and given forth again with its particular—and often complex—emotional value. But it is to be noted that, again like Proust, Katherine Mansfield orders her impressions until they form an artistic whole. [It is perhaps worth noting too, that the tale *A Married Man's Story* is somewhat like Proust in manner, in method of approach.] But the important thing is that in her work along with the sensibility there is a definite intellectual control. This is very apparent when the story has arisen out of some intimate personal experience; for example, the mental agony recorded in the *Journal* entry of January 1920 is obviously connected with the story *The Man without a Temperament* which was worked out at this time and of which the origin is clearly to be found in Katherine Mansfield's own life.

All her work from the earliest stories shows this maturity, this clear and unfumbling knowledge of what she is doing. Often the idea to be conveyed, the feeling to be communicated, is done as it were aside, with a subtle touch which gives a new freshness and clarity to the meaning; but it is never done unconsciously. The medium of expression is always equal to what has to be expressed. The little sketch called *The Samuel Josephs*, for example, seems to be an earlier version of part of the theme of *Prelude*. Except for the omission of one longish scene with the Samuel Josephs at play, which in itself is excellent and may well have been reserved for later use, the changes that take place in the later version are very few. A word or phrase is altered to sharpen the impression and make it more vivid, and there is the significant omission of two paragraphs which are less concrete, more loose and spread than the rest. Or again, compare any of the tales in *Something Childish but very Natural* with any of those in the last book, *The Dove's Nest*. The effects, it is true, in the latter case, are obtained by fewer strokes, but the essential quality of the writing is the same. The stories when she begins writing have a practically perfect technique; when she finishes, the technique is quite perfect. The advance is simply one of elimination—of suppressing everything that is not completely necessary for the purposes of the story. This perfection of technique is in itself a danger, and some of the later tales are *tours de force*. The risk in short-story writing is of letting the tale become a "situation"; that is, of letting the arrangement of the movement, the crisis, of the tale supersede its significance. This is what happens in the well-managed story *Bliss*, and again in *A Cup of Tea*; the structure is so perfect that one does not realize at first that it is artificial. But this was not what Katherine Mansfield was most concerned with and she realized the difficulty—two stories (*Widowed*, and *Second Violin*, of which only fragments remain) were abandoned by her because they "felt betrayed." What she *was* concerned with was something very different from situation or effect.

Her notion of art was something supremely difficult and supremely simple. In the *Journal* 1921 she writes, "To me, life and work are two things indivisible. It's only by being true to life that I can be true to art. And to be true to life is to be *good, sincere, simple, honest*." How close a connection art and life had for her is revealed by the *Journal*, and how agonizing. But it is to be noted that it is not the emotions of the writer that are obtruded in her work. The third outstanding characteristic of the tales is their objectivity. She remarks in the *Journal*, "One must learn, one must practise to *forget* oneself. I can't tell the truth about . . . unless I am free to look into her life without self-consciousness." In this she is noticeably different from the school of writers characterized best by Virginia Woolf and E. M. Forster, whose works, in spite of the figures that obtain life in them, are essentially (as for instance in *The Waves*) records of different aspects of the author's personality. What one obtains most strongly through the people and events there shown, is the impression of a definite expression of temperament, of a considered or unconscious judgment. Katherine Mansfield's work was of the opposite, in intention and effect. She has accepted life; compare the agonizing pages in the *Journal* of 1920. "There is no limit to human suffering. . . . What must one do? There is no question of 'passing beyond it.' This is false. One must submit. Do not resist. Take it. Be overwhelmed. Accept it fully. Make it part of life. . . . The fearful pain will fade. I must turn to work. I must put my agony into something, change it."

This acceptance of life in its entirety is perhaps the key to her work, which includes, in its sympathetic and penetrating observation, characters widely divergent both in accidentals, and in temperament and feeling. What she records, truthfully and omitting nothing that is relevant, are the different phases of life that have struck her consciousness. Perhaps the best example to point this statement is the story called *The Young Girl*, an impressionistic sketch which is imaginatively true—the origin of the tale is probably to be found in the *Journal* entry of April 12, 1920, and indicates from what slight impressions the completed effect is produced. The value lies both in the depth and sensitiveness of the impression and in the imaginative comprehension with which it is re-built.

Yet is it enough to say that by her art she recorded, at once delicately and with strength, impressions of life snatched from time and made, by the exquisite responsiveness of her style, to re-live? It is somehow too cold a judgment. In the tales which represent her genius best, in *The Doll's House*, in *Prelude*, in *At the Bay*, there is something more than this. These tales are indubitably of the highest order; had she lived one may speculate that she would have produced work like this in quality if not in subject. The difference between them and the other tales is one of more intense feeling. They are all concerned with the life which she had known so vividly in New Zealand in her childhood, and perhaps because she knew she was now cut off from it, she has made it re-live in a way in which none of the other tales do. It is a tribute to the objectivity of her art, and to its power, that the personal loss which forced her to begin the tales has resulted in this un-selfconscious, comprehending participation.

Perhaps *At the Bay* is the more rounded and complete. In the limits of one day various episodes in the life of the Burnell family are presented to us, so vividly and naturally that the people become alive, from Pat the handyman and Alice the servant-girl to Kezia and her grandmother. But the importance lies not in the episodes taken by themselves, but in the subtle way in which they form a whole, at once real and significant. It is very remarkable that in her later work what becomes more and more stressed is not the incident or episode in itself but its implication of the life outside it. *The Doll's House*, in its exquisite and tender feeling, is much more than a piece of childhood re-caught. And so in *Prelude*, which is perhaps the best tale she wrote, through the life of the family in its variety and reality of detail we obtain an impression of life itself, in its ugliness, humour, pathos, weakness, and beauty. The medium of communication—that clear delicate prose which can express, and both unforgettably, the lyric freshness of early morning and the complicated play of character, is here seen at its height. Partly because of the delicacy of interpretation, partly because of the strength of feeling, these tales have in great measure the effect of poetry. All is suffused in a warm tender light, a light that reveals, and illuminates.

Printed in Great Britain
by T. and A. Constable Ltd.
at the University Press
Edinburgh